# HOLY LIVING IN AN UNHOLY WORLD

# Holy Living in an Unholy World

*Balancing Love, Law, and Grace*

Erwin W. Lutzer

Moody Church Media
Chicago

*Cover by Bryan Butler*

Revised and expanded.
Originally published in 1974 as *How In This World Can I Be Holy?*

**HOLY LIVING IN AN UNHOLY WORLD**
Copyright © 2023 by Erwin W. Lutzer
Published by Moody Church Media
Chicago, Illinois 60614
www.moodymedia.org

ISBN: 9798387188893

**Dedication**

To my wife, Rebecca Anne,
whose unselfish concern for others sets her apart
from the value system of our fallen world.

**Acknowledgments**

I still have much appreciation for the late
Dr. Charles Ryrie who wrote the foreword
and offered his personal encouragement when I first
published this work back in 1974.

# CONTENTS

ERWIN W. LUTZER

# FOREWORD

This is a book that needed to be written. Its message comes through loud and clear. It is a sober call to holiness and to total commitment to the Lord. And in the process, it demolishes many evangelical sacred cows of Christian living.

Mr. Lutzer, already known to many by his first book, *The Morality Gap,* turns his attention in this work to a consideration of how to be in the world but not of it. His writing is clear; his illustrations to the point; his analyses penetrating. Anyone who thinks he will see only the faults of others in these pages will not have to read very far before seeing himself.

Seldom are the aspects of true spirituality treated in as unbiased a way as they are in this book. Take the subject of legalism, for instance. How often the word is used; how seldom it is defined; how rarely it is applied correctly. Or take the matter of doctrinal separation. How should it be balanced with the doctrine of the unity of the Body of Christ? Or worldliness—which is usually described in terms of what others do that I don't approve of. This book knocks down rules and supports them, and both opposite actions are properly described.

Above all, the book is biblical. More than once, I stopped my reading to begin to debate with the author, but soon I realized he was pointing me to the truths of the Scriptures. Where the Bible does not speak directly about matters he discusses, the author is careful to be guided by scriptural principles of holiness. It is a genuine privilege to commend this book to all in the family of God who aspire to biblical holiness.

Charles C. Ryrie

CHAPTER ONE

# YOU IN THE WORLD

Søren Kierkegaard, the Danish theologian and philosopher, told this parable: A wild duck was flying northward with his mate across Europe during the springtime. En route, he happened to land in a barnyard in Denmark, where he quickly made friends with the tame ducks that lived there. The wild duck enjoyed the corn and fresh water. He decided to stay for an hour, then for a day, then for a week, and finally, for a month. At the end of that time, he contemplated flying to join his friends in the vast Northland, but he had begun to enjoy the safety of the barnyard, and the tame ducks had made him feel welcome. So he stayed on for the summer.

One autumn day, when his wild mates were flying toward the south, he heard their quacking. It stirred him with delight, and he enthusiastically flapped his wings and rose into the air to join them. Much to his dismay, he found that he could rise no higher than the eaves of the barn. As he waddled back to the safety of the barnyard, he muttered to himself, "I'm satisfied here. I have plenty of food, and the fare is good. Why should I leave?" So, he spent the winter on the farm.

In the spring, when the wild ducks flew overhead again, he felt a strange stirring within his breast, but he didn't even try to fly up to meet them. When they returned in the fall, they again invited him to rejoin them, but this time, the duck didn't even notice them. There was no stirring within his breast. He simply kept on eating the corn which had made him fat.

Today, we face a challenge. It is the challenge of abandoning the security of worldly attitudes and lifestyles to be free from the gravitational pull of the world. It is the challenge of choosing the hard path even when an easy one is open to us. It is the challenge of living supernaturally. It is the invitation to lose our life in order to find it.

Some of us will turn a deaf ear to our calling. Many will sense only a faint stirring within when they learn what Christ expects. For a fleeting moment, they will feel the impulse to walk in newness of life. But the comforts of the world, the pressures of their occupation, and the love of luxury will keep them bound to the world. They are satisfied with themselves. They will stay where they are.

Others will try to rise above their present commitment. They will free themselves from the attraction of money, status, and self-satisfaction. They will turn over a new leaf, make fresh promises, and determine to live a dedicated life. But they will not rise very high. Their dreams will lie buried beneath the fear that the cost is too great. They will walk slowly back to the security of former ways.

Fortunately, we find that others—perhaps only a few—will rise above their complacent friends. They will feel a tug toward the world, but they will be drawn toward heaven too. They will not be satisfied by satiating themselves with the luxury, pleasure, and status-conscious value system of the "religious" community. They will turn from security to exposure, from contentment to a gnawing hunger, and from prejudice to love. They will begin to serve one Master rather than two. And unlike the wild duck of Denmark, they will fly!

However, changing our lifestyle is painful, threatening, and often humiliating. It necessitates the delicate task of being *in* the world though not *of* it. It also involves an evaluation of ourselves, an evaluation that penetrates the hidden thoughts and secret motivations of our hearts.

When we knowingly adopt the lifestyle of the world, we have the option of abandoning our values to live a life of radical commitment to Jesus Christ. But tragically, many Christians have accepted worldly attitudes without even being aware of it. They cannot have their lives changed, because they sense no need for inward renewal. They have not awakened from the peaceful slumber of self-righteousness. They have yet to realize that a person may give money to the church; abstain from substance abuse and pornography; win awards for Sunday school attendance; be scrupulous in conduct, and at the same time, they can be worldly to the core.

Oddly enough, those of us who have had biblical training often find it most difficult to evaluate ourselves. The Pharisees, who knew the law and did their best to live by it, were further from the kingdom than the tax collectors and prostitutes (Matthew 21:31). It could be that great sinners are more conscious of their need for God's mercy than the self-righteous. Perhaps some of us have even eliminated our need of God. More of that later.

Living in the world is not easy. Take conduct, for example. A generation ago, many Christians simply assumed certain amusements, entertainment, and fashions were not acceptable for them. Some churches published lists of sins to be avoided. Members in good standing conformed to the list and expected their children to do the same.

This method of solving questions of conduct had the advantage of being simple and clear-cut. The boundary between Christian conduct and worldliness was drawn with some degree of precision, and a Christian could simply follow the expected pattern.

Perceptive Christians, however, noticed some contradictions between the various sins associated with worldliness; in other instances, they made hair-splitting distinctions that could not be defended. Furthermore, standards varied from denomination to denomination, church to church, and from state to state. As a result, many questioned whether we had found *God's* standards or whether we were following the opinion of fallible men.

Interestingly, this generation of Christians condones what the past generation condemned. Many Christians were opposed to televisions in the homes back in the 1950s. Today, Christians have more than one television set in their homes, plus multiple ways to watch programs from smartphones to laptop computers. Sunday sports were condemned a generation ago; today Christian athletes, who play on Sunday, are heroes in the Christian community. Back in the 1960s and 70s, a typical Christian was defined as one who saw his movies twenty years after they were released. Now that attending movies is no longer taboo, and in fact, can be watched on your smartphone at any time of the day or night, that definition can be discarded. At any rate, neat distinctions between good and evil vanished with the horse and buggy.

Even among non-Christians just a couple of generations ago, there was more agreement regarding right and wrong, or at least between what was *considered* right or wrong.

Today, many of these "old" views are being questioned and even rejected. The black and white of yesterday has dissolved into a blurred gray of today.

With new forms of amusement being invented, and with changes in the moral climate being greeted with indifference by many Christians, we can't possibly predict what might be acceptable Christian conduct in the future. Someone has observed that time is the great sanctifier. The "sin" of today becomes acceptable tomorrow.

A factory official phoned a news bureau every morning to set the factory clocks to conform to the clocks at the bureau office. But when the noon whistle of the factory blew, the head of the bureau changed their clocks to agree with the whistle. The factory depended on the bureau and the bureau on the factory. Neither set its clocks by an objective standard. Likewise, the standards Christians accept today are often those of the local Christian community. But the standards of the Christian community are merely the product of local Christians. When we superficially compare ourselves with ourselves, since we create our own standards, we can gleefully give ourselves a passing grade. We are like the four-year-old boy who announced to his mother, "I'm seven feet tall." And he was right—according to the yardstick *he* had made.

Where will all the discussion on proper Christian conduct end? Perhaps that question cannot be answered apart from a more fundamental one, namely, where did it all begin? Surely God's standards have not changed. Why then have we become trapped in inconsistencies and contradictions? Why has no agreement ever been reached as to which list of sins is complete? Perhaps it's because our view of worldliness is too shallow—or too unbiblical. Maybe we have strained at a gnat and have swallowed a camel. Maybe.

What should our attitude be toward the modern trends hammering away at the accepted standards of the past? Does the Bible have anything to say about these matters? Could it be we must reexamine principles of Christian conduct that will deliver us from simply accepting the standards of the world in the future?

Questions of conduct also force us to reflect on how we should relate to other Christians. What should be our attitude toward Christians whose lifestyles differ from ours? Or whose doctrinal views don't coincide with ours?

Our relationship with society presents its own difficulties. On one hand, we are not to be drawn into sin; yet we are also to befriend unbelievers. Many Christians think it's impossible to do both. As a result, they have withdrawn from the non-Christian community. They transfer to the sinner their supposed hatred for sin. They would prefer not even knowing their neighbors' names, let alone trying to love them as they love themselves. But before we wash our hands of direct personal involvement, before we shirk our social responsibility under the guise of preaching the gospel, we must take another look at what it means to do good to all men—even to those who are not of the household of faith. Maybe we even have to rethink our understanding of the total biblical message and its implications for the social needs of today.

Jesus prayed that His followers, remaining *in* the world though not *of* it, might not be overcome by the world. What this means specifically has been discussed and debated. Some Christians tell us we should become more involved in the world; others, believing Christians are too worldly already, argue for more separation. Some isolate themselves from non-Christians in order to maintain purity; others have participated in doubtful activities to win souls to Christ. A growing number of Christians work toward church unity; others are opposed to it, and a good number are indifferent. Hopefully this book will shed light on these matters.

Also, this book is a call to a commitment to rise above the perceived humdrum of traditional Christianity. It's a call to march to a different drummer and to be out of step with the world.

To be holy in heaven will not be difficult. It will be the only life possible. To be holy in the world, however, is another matter. Here we feel the pressure of the world, the flesh, and the devil. Yet we are to live in the world without being contaminated by it. Heaven is not the problem; it is here on Earth that we face our most difficult assignment. As the anonymous jingle puts it:

> To live above with the saints I love,
>
> Oh, that will be glory.
>
> But to live below with the saints I know—
>
> Well, that's another story.

This other story is what this book is about: Saints living with other saints in a world of luxury, pleasure, and moral decay. Living in this world is difficult enough, but the crucial question is: How can we live holy lives in an unholy world? This question cannot be answered thoughtlessly. We shall consider it in the following chapters.

## QUESTIONS FOR DISCUSSION

1. Discuss the problem of being in the world though not of it. What challenge does the Christian face in this regard?

2. What are the dangers of adopting worldly attitudes and lifestyles?

3. Discuss the difference between Christian conduct and worldliness. What should be our attitude toward modern trends of conduct that conflict with accepted standards of the past?

ERWIN W. LUTZER

CHAPTER TWO

# THE WORLD: A PUZZLE WITH FOUR PIECES

A mother was choosing a gift for her son. "That's a rather complicated toy for a six-year-old, isn't it?" she asked. The clerk nodded, "Yes, it is. But this toy is designed to teach your child to live in this world, because no matter how he puts it together, it will always come out wrong!"

How true! We are living in a world where nothing turns out quite right. The cars and planes that have made travel swift and enjoyable have also polluted the air we breathe. Our big cities suffocate in the smog created by our own technology. The world's natural resources are being depleted to keep up with the hunger for new technologies and innovations. Our lakes, rivers, and oceans are contaminated with waste from factories and our own trash.

We have put men on the moon but haven't found a solution for moral decay. We have made gigantic strides in medicine but can't stop the alarming number of divorces and the near dissolution of the family unit. Technology has given us more leisure time, but with it has come boredom and meaninglessness.

Novelist Ayn Rand, in an interview with college students, was asked, "What's wrong with our world?" She summed it up this way: "Never before has the world been so desperately asking for answers to crucial questions, and never before has the world been so frantically committed to the idea that no answers are possible. To paraphrase the Bible, the modern attitude is 'Father, forgive us for we know not what we are doing—and please don't tell us!'"[1] Like Humpty Dumpty, the world has come apart, and all the king's horses and all the king's men cannot put it back together again. As Christians, our tension is compounded because we are citizens of heaven as well as the world.

The term *worldliness* is often used to describe attitudes and conduct opposed to God's will. James wrote that friendship with the world is hostility toward God (James 4:4). Christians are in the world but are not to be like the world (worldly).

In order to shun worldliness, we must know what it is and what it is not. Are those who are concerned about ecology worldly? What about the not-so-obvious worldly areas of our lives: fashion, art, music, and techology? What place should they have in the Christian's life? Should worldliness be defined in terms of *what* we do, *why* we do it, or both? We can only begin to grapple with such questions when we sort out the pieces of the world's puzzle.

To clarify our thinking, we must distinguish between three uses of the word *world* in Scripture. Sometimes it refers to this planet and therefore has implications for ecology and aesthetic beauty. The same word is also used to refer to the whole human race. This relationship to the world of people is crucial in pinpointing our role in Christian living. Then often, the word *world* refers to the system of values and attitudes accepted by a society which has abandoned God. These distinctions will help us identify what part of the world we should hate, what part we should love, and how we can distinguish between the two.

## THE WORLD AS A PLANET

When God created the world (planet), He pronounced it "good" (Genesis 1:10). We can't visualize what Earth looked like initially, but we know that it was both beautiful and adequate for the physical needs of people and animals. When Adam and Eve were created, God gave them authority over the planet with its animals and vegetation. After sin entered, God did not revoke mankind's authority. Today, mankind has a legitimate right to rule over the planet and to use it for his comfort, food, and enjoyment.

This original mandate is directly related to the ecological imbalance we face today. Christians often display little concern about our ecological problem because the coming of Christ is believed to be near. Since the present world is only temporary, it would seem that a lack of concern is justified. But is it? What is implied by the command God gave to Adam? Do we have license to do as we wish with the planet, or should we be concerned about the use (or misuse) of natural resources?

One member of a televised panel discussion stated flatly, "Our ecological crises can be blamed on the Bible. God gave man authority over the earth—authority to squander its resources." He went on to say that the answer to our ecological dilemmas is to realize that nature is, in fact, God. Presumably, if the world is but an extension of the essence of God, then man will respect nature. To hurt nature will be to hurt God.

Is pantheism (the doctrine that nature is God) the answer to man's tendency to misuse natural resources? Albert Schweitzer believed nature was God and, as a result, refused to kill flies and mosquitoes. He thought that if nature is God, he had no right to fight nature. However, if he had been more consistent, he would not have killed germs either.

The pantheist faces the problem raised by Albert Camus in his book, *The Plague*. In the story, the rat-catcher faces a dilemma: If he joins the doctors and fights the plague, he fights against God; if he does not fight the plague, he is not being humanitarian. The pantheist cannot fight the plague.

Remember, to fight nature is to fight God.

Furthermore, if there is no personal God, then nature is only the product of time plus chance. It is the result of blind and unintelligent forces acting together without aim or purpose. If this is true, why should we treat a tree—or for that matter, a person—with dignity? Pantheism cannot be the answer to our ecological dilemma. It can't tell us why we should fight nature's harmful side, nor can it give us a reason to treat any part of nature with respect.

The biblical view of creation puts ecology in proper perspective. God's command to Adam and Eve didn't give them license to treat the planet with disrespect. Mankind was made a steward over it and, therefore, is responsible for the care of the environment. Earth remains God's possession. Man was appointed caretaker until Christ comes to rule it. Mankind is, therefore, accountable to God for the temporary mandate given him. As with the gifts of life, money, and time, we will answer to God for our stewardship of the planet.

Concern about ecology is not worldliness; it is wise stewardship. But our concern becomes misguided when it overshadows the weightier matters of God's will. Non-Christians can also lead the fight against pollution and the careless use of Earth's resources and today, it has become a mantra for many in political power—even used to justify irrational laws or proposals that will "save the planet."

Ecology should not be anyone's primary focus. Though it is a part of God's plan for us, it is only a part. To give it its rightful place, we should personally and corporately do whatever we can to prevent the misuse of God's Earth. We cannot ignore the planet without slighting its Maker.

However, there is another aspect of the world that should be higher on our list of priorities than the resources of this planet. It is more important than rivers, trees, and clean air. When we love this aspect of the world, we love what God loves.

## THE WORLD OF PEOPLE

Charles Schultz, in his comic strip, "Peanuts," depicts Linus asking Charlie Brown, "What do you plan to be?" He replies, "A doctor." Linus responds, "You can't be a doctor because you don't love humanity." Charlie Brown is taken by surprise. "I do love humanity; it's just the people that I can't stand!"

I can identify with Charlie Brown. Being concerned about humanity is one thing; loving people is another.

As a young man, I promised myself that I would never become the pastor of a church because I was frightened at the prospect of facing real problems. Teaching in a college was easy: almost all of the answers could be found in textbooks. But shattered marriages, discipline problems, and personality clashes were in a different category. There are no quick solutions to human needs, yet helping people is what followers of Christ are to do.

Even after pastoring The Moody Church for 36 years and becoming Pastor Emeritus, I'm still learning. I'm learning that God often calls us to do the impossible (like being a pastor, for instance!). I'm learning that difficulties in our lives and the lives of others are designed to teach us the need for rich qualities of character and love.

Christ's primary concern is for the world of people. It is this world we should love supremely. But it's not easy.

It's easy for me to like the neighbors who live next door to me and my wife. They are trustworthy, kind, and quiet. They never meddle in our affairs, and we return the compliment. However, can I say that I love them as myself? There is plenty of room for improvement.

It's even harder to love those who keep us awake at night or pester us with frequent visits. Sometimes, love becomes more difficult in proportion to the amount of contact we have with certain friends or enemies. Even obnoxious friends can be loved if they visit us only once a year. Yet Jesus said we are to love both our neighbors and enemies, maybe because He realized they were often the same people!

Consider this: Could you love someone who killed your wife and father? Kim Joon-gon did. He pleaded with a judge to spare the life of the Communists in Korea who committed the murders, because, "The Lord, whose I am and whom I serve would have me show mercy to them." Later, he led them to Christ. That is love.

Jesus did not die for a select few but became the sacrifice for the sins of the whole world (1 John 2:2). God loves the Communists, Nazis, Democrats, and Republicans. He loves the world.

Friends and relatives who appreciate us are easily loved; but to love those who hate us is asking too much, especially if they dislike us for no apparent reason. Yet Jesus asked the penetrating question, "For if you love those who love you, what reward do you have? Do not even the tax collectors do the same?" (Matthew 5:46). His point is clear: We can love those who love us and yet be distinctly worldly. There is nothing unique about loving those who attend our church or those who compliment us for our ingenuity. That kind of love exists in all societies, Christian and non-Christian alike. To love without receiving love in return, to love without racial prejudice, to love our enemies, that is what Christ demands.

When we think of God's love for the world, we often imagine that His love is directed to an undifferentiated mass of humanity. It's hard to grasp the notion that each of the more than eight billion people in the world is loved personally. We are not datapoints in a computer.

My wife and I, with some friends, were driving past a

cemetery. "My husband and I bought our grave plots over there," the woman said, pointing beyond a grove of trees. Then she added, "Do you think that God will remember where we are buried in the day of resurrection?" This woman was not seriously questioning God's knowledge nor His ability to remember. She was looking for the reassurance that she meant something—something very important—to God. In our depersonalized society, people have the need to feel loved, wanted, and remembered. Jesus, our Good Shepherd, calls His own sheep by *name* and leads them out (John 10:3). The personal element is always there.

That's the pattern for us to follow in our love for others. Each of us needs the assurance that someone cares about *us*. Children deprived of love often display emotional stress or deviant behavior patterns. Adults who are unloved experience futility and hatred toward society. Many are incapable of showing love themselves, yet they need someone to love them without expecting anything in return.

I have found that loving others takes effort and time. If each one of us would determine to go the first mile (not to mention the second) for someone else each week, this could be the beginning of meaningful involvement in the lives of others.

It's good for us to remember that to despise people is to despise God. Whether we are in the world or of it can largely be determined by our response to our neighbor—

especially the neighbor who has wronged us.

The implications of concern for others will be spelled out in later chapters. For now, we should remember we have the opportunity to serve God when we serve people. If, like Charlie Brown, we love humanity in general but dislike people in particular, we have not become properly adjusted to the world.

God loved the world. Go thou, and do likewise.

## THE WORLD SYSTEM

Two thieves who broke into a clothing store had a bit of fun before their successful escape. They rearranged the price tags on many of the items for sale. The next morning, customers noticed that suits were priced at five dollars each and shoes were several hundred dollars. The thieves couldn't change the value of the merchandise, but changing the price tags was relatively simple.

What is worldliness? It is living with warped values. At its worst, worldliness is assigning value to what God totally condemns; at its best, it's rearranging the price tags to fit our wants and desires. It's rejecting God's priorities and substituting our own. Here are three of the most common areas where God's priorities are replaced by ours.

The first is the area of sensual pleasure. God has made provision for the fulfillment of sexual drives within marriage. Yet in our society, sexual fulfillment is given emphasis while sexual restraint is viewed with suspicion. Movies, books, and sleek magazines and websites continually suggest that the answer to boredom and meaninglessness is to have an affair with a good sex partner. Marriages fall apart because one partner believes they are missing out on some sensual pleasure a different sex partner would bring. Yet those who buy this theory never find that ultimate fulfillment which our sex-saturated society promises.

God's plan is that sex should be part of life, but it should not be the primary criterion for happiness. Many happy marriages exist without sexual enjoyment as the basis. Single adults who do not engage in sexual activities are able to live happy and meaningful lives, as the apostle Paul suggested (1 Corinthians 7:8).

Before Adam and Eve sinned, God blessed the sexual relationship. The first sin was not the sex act, as some theologians have suggested. Sex within God's parameters has His full approval. Sin, however, distorts the drives created by God. Love turns to lust, monogamy turns to polygamy, and freedom turns to sensual slavery.

The lust of the flesh, a characteristic of worldliness, refers to any sensual pleasure severed from God's intended purpose. That pleasure can be overt, or it can be only in the mind. Worldliness is not just doing what's forbidden but also wishing we could do it. One of its distinctives is mental slavery to illegitimate pleasure. Worldliness twists values by rearranging their price tags.

The second area is a direct violation of the tenth commandment. Listen to any casual conversation in a store or at a lunch break, and you will discover that the discussion is usually about money or the things it can buy. The topic usually is new clothes, cars, furniture, or houses. What one person buys another covets.

Almost all advertising is based on covetousness. Ads feature glamorous young women and handsome men trying to convince us that we can be as happy as they are if we buy a certain product. Beyond this deception, there is an even more subtle philosophy: We should not be happy with what we have. To the advertising industry, being content is a cardinal sin. If we are satisfied with our present vacuum cleaner, we won't buy a new one. So we are bombarded with advertisements designed to make us dissatisfied with our current television, our outdated suits or jeans, even our favorite mouthwash.

Mass media, especially the internet with its on-demand availability of anything you want to watch, read, or buy, has made us conscious of our own peculiarities. We are told which fashions, hairstyles, and home decor are in and which ones are obsolete. The hallmark of the advertising industry is conformity: Everyone should wear the same designer clothes, drive a new car, and drink the same soft drink. Soon we begin to compare ourselves with others who have more than we do (which is more popular than comparing ourselves with those who have less). As a result, we are dissatisfied, status-conscious, and ungrateful. Our relationship with God is choked, and we become hooked on the world.

Covetousness is so subtle because we do need money, cars, and clothes. Furthermore, luxuries are not sinful in themselves. Therefore, we easily justify our greed under the legitimate guise of "making a living."

There is another side to covetousness. It's not just a matter of wanting the latest and greatest, it also involves being ungrateful for what we have. Complaining about our lot in life might seem quite innocent in itself, but God takes it personally. When the Israelites resented the desert and the quality of their food, they directed their criticism to Moses, but the Lord said it was really a complaint against the Almighty Himself.

When we are not content with what we have, when we envy those who have more than we do, we have adopted the attitude of the world. Covetousness is a trademark of worldliness. It puts a high premium on second-rate values.

The third area where our worldliness corrupts God's design is our self-image. God created us with the need to feel wanted and accepted among our friends. But sin perverts all facets of our value system. Legitimate needs are twisted into illegitimate passions. So it is with what the apostle John calls the pride of life (1 John 2:16). Pride is the sin of taking credit for something someone else has done. We have our parents to thank if we have exceptional physical beauty, for instance. And since there is nothing we can do apart from God who gives us health, strength, and ability, it is sin to think ourselves better than others because of what *we* have done.

Let's suppose we are successful but our neighbor is not. Or let's assume we have more ability, intelligence, and influence. Do we consider ourselves more worthy of God's blessings? If so, that is pride.

In contrast, humility is not deceitfulness regarding what God has given to us. Humility is evaluating ourselves correctly; it is knowing both our strengths and our weaknesses. It is seeing ourselves in proper perspective, and if we have been successful (whatever that might mean in a Christian context), humility is consciously giving all of the credit to God.

Humility is characterized by personal security; it means we will not be jealous of other people's success or resentful if they do in one year what we could not achieve in five. A humble person will never find fault with another simply to satisfy the desire for personal gratification. Nor will he refuse to become involved, under the pretense of being inferior.

On the other hand, pride produces insecurity. It

magnifies the desire for recognition and influence and enlarges personal ambition beyond reason. Pride demands that we get even with those who have wronged us; it turns love into bitterness.

Whenever we pretend to be what we really are not, or when we are motivated by the insatiable thirst for recognition, we have been gripped by the pride of life. The real need for acceptance has been turned into the bondage of selfish desire.

## PUTTING IT ALL TOGETHER

Think back over the three *worlds* we have talked about. When God created Adam and Eve, they were to be properly adjusted to these three aspects of the world. God commanded them to take care of the garden and to have dominion over the earth. Mankind was meant to subdue, or control, this *planet.*

God also provided Adam with a wife because humans were created to be a social creatures who desired companionship. In the person of his wife and later his children, Adam was introduced to the world of society.

After Adam and Eve ate of the forbidden fruit, their world received an added dimension. Sin warped their attitudes and twisted their desires. The world as a system was born.

Yet another devastating consequence also resulted:

humanity was cut off from God. No longer could Adam walk with the Almighty in the cool of the day. In a word, man was lost.

Ever since that day in Eden, we have tried to adjust to the three aspects of the world, but we can't do so on our own. To be adjusted to our surroundings, to be rightly related to society, and to be delivered from our sinful impulses, requires supernatural help.

Therefore, the fourth piece of the puzzle is our spiritual world—the vacuum in our spirits which can only be filled by the Creator. Whether we are worldly or not depends on what (or who) satisfies the deep needs within us. Is it God? Or our own ambitions?

Worldliness is excluding God from our lives and, therefore, consciously or unconsciously, accepting the values of a man-centered society. Sometimes it involves committing overt sins for immediate gratification, but more often, for Christians, it simply means living as though this world—*our* world—is all that matters. It's letting our job, leisure time, home, and church rotate around our special interests, pleasures, and secret satisfactions. It's spending our time to serve ourselves rather than others; it's arranging our priorities with ourselves in mind; it's living as though God doesn't really matter in everyday life. It is changing God's price tags.

Worldly attitudes never lead us to where we think

we're going. We seek pleasure but are never happy; we buy things but are never satisfied; we attain success but never find fulfillment.

Ironically, we are able to find what we seek if we look for it in a different direction. When we seek first the kingdom of God and righteousness, fulfillment comes as a byproduct of our love for God. And that satisfaction is better than we ever imagined. God can make the pieces of this world's puzzle fit together; He helps us view the world from a new perspective.

If worldliness is living with wrong attitudes and values, the cure is to rearrange our priorities to comply with God's blueprint. Living within the world without being contaminated by it will involve negative laws as well as positive commands. It will take wisdom, determination, and supernatural power. Our present schedules might have to be altered and our desires changed.

In order to narrow the scope of this book, I have omitted any further discussion of our relationship to the world as a planet. The rest of this book is an attempt to discuss our relationship to (1) the world of people, (2) the world system, and (3) God.

## QUESTIONS FOR DISCUSSION

1. Read James 4:4. What is James' definition of worldliness?
2. Describe the three uses of the word *world* in Scripture.

3. Which of the three worlds is Christ's primary concern? Why?

4. Read Matthew 5:46. What point was Jesus making?

5. What is meant by the phrase "world system"?

6. In what three areas do we commonly replace God's priorities with ours?

7. How can we best adjust ourselves to the three aspects of the world?

# PART I

# LIVING IN
# THE WORLD OF PEOPLE

ERWIN W. LUTZER

CHAPTER THREE

# CONTACT WITHOUT CONTAMINATION

In the Middle Ages, monasteries were built to keep the monks separate from the influence of the world. The theory was that if they didn't associate with those who sinned, then they could attain holiness.

To a limited degree, this notion is still alive today. Christian parents often assume their children will escape the evil of the world by being kept from knowing about certain sins or by attending a Christian school where evil might be less common. Without question, this has some merit. In the Old Testament, God commanded the Israelites to be physically separate from the Canaanites, lest the nation follow foreign gods. But those who have depended on a Christian environment to produce holiness (and thereby negate the evil influence of the world) have often been rudely awakened by the realization that spirituality is not automatically produced by Christian surroundings any more than motorcycles are transformed into cars by being put into a garage. Something more fundamental must take place in an individual's life in order to become holy. A Christian environment should encourage godliness, but it cannot guarantee it.

The other extreme is to assume we must participate in all the activities of non-Christians in order to share the gospel with them. Some Christians think it's necessary to drink liquor to witness to an alcoholic; others attend movies or read literature of questionable moral content in order to relate the biblical message effectively to the needs of today. One Christian girl planned to become a Playboy Bunny in order to win other bunnies (presumably).

How can we find a balance—if there is one—between the two extremes? What is separation all about? Perhaps the life of Jesus provides a clue to true separation. Of His followers, He said, "They are not of the world, *just as I am not of the world*" (John 17:16, italics added). As He *was*, so we *should be*.

## PERSONAL INSULATION

Regardless of how we define Christ's separation from the world, one fact is clear: He did not separate Himself from human beings and their needs. Nor did He limit His concern to the spiritual part of a person's personality. When He saw the multitude, He was moved with compassion toward them. He not only saw the value of their souls but saw their physical and emotional needs as well (Matthew 9:35–36). Jesus was concerned about the *whole* person, and His words matched His actions.

Jesus displayed love by healing numerous people. He didn't merely give them the gospel then move on to His next appointment, but rather He used physical healings as an illustration of the goodness of God in granting forgiveness, pardon, and peace (Mark 2:10).

In the parable of the Good Samaritan, Jesus commended the Samaritan for making an effort to help the wounded stranger. If the Samaritan had been concerned about souls and not bodies, it would have been possible for him to rationalize (as the priest and Levite did) that he too should pass by on the other side. But unlike the religious leaders, the Samaritan realized that loving one's neighbor means helping a stranger who has been wounded—even when it is risky. Evidently, the Samaritan didn't try to explain his religious beliefs to the wounded man (at least Jesus doesn't mention it in the parable); yet the Samaritan was commended for helping a man in physical need. A man's body is important in the sight of God, and our response to others in their physical need becomes the real test of loving our neighbors as ourselves.

Obviously, the message of salvation would have been meaningless to this beaten man if it had come through the lips of the priest or the Levite, who didn't care about his aches, pains, and wounds. Certainly the primary responsibility of the Christian is to share the gospel and make disciples of all nations. But this will not be done (nor can it be done) by those who share the gospel verbally but show no concern for individuals as *whole* persons. People respond more readily when they sense someone is concerned about their physical and emotional needs. This prepares them to accept the spiritual dimension of the Christian message. If we treat non-Christians as if they are unimportant but their soul (the invisible, intangible, and elusive part of them) is important, they won't believe we are really concerned about them. They will suspect we have befriended them only for "religious" purposes, which may drive them away from the gospel message. A genuine concern for their mental, emotional, and physical well-being can be the means God will use to draw them to Himself.

Jesus also disregarded social barriers. In the parable of the Good Samaritan, He deliberately chose to honor a man of a despised race—a Samaritan. During the time of Jesus, Samaritans were despised by the Jews. Knowing this hatred, when Jesus asked the lawyer, "Which of these three, do you think, proved to be a neighbor to the man who fell among the robbers?" (Luke 10:36), the Jewish lawyer probably didn't want to use the word *Samaritan*, and so replied, "The one who showed him mercy" (v. 37).

Jesus could have avoided Samaria as the religious leaders of His time did, but He did not show partiality. Unlike some churches, His ministry was not segregated; He deliberately went out of His way to make sure of it.

It is much easier to talk about the unity of the body of Christ than to practice it. Yet the uniqueness of the Christian church should be its loving unity despite racial and economic diversity. When Christians choose a church because of its racial or social atmosphere, they are adopting the attitude of the world. The fact that a group of middle-class dentists is able to get along together is not really unique. Members of community clubs are able to coexist without great effort as they share the same background and social status. But the Christian church was designed to have unity despite color, race, or differing income levels. It's a pity that secular social organizations have often been more willing to accept minority groups than some Christian churches.

Jesus didn't respect social status—He never courted the rich. In fact, the opposite was true. The rich came to Him (Matthew 27:57; Mark 10:17–22), but He went to the poor (Matthew 11:5; Mark 12:37). In the book of James, worldliness is explicitly defined as an attitude of personal favoritism (1:27; 2:1). In some churches, those dressed in expensive clothes are treated with greater respect than the poor dressed in rags. James reminds his readers that God chose the poor of this world to be rich in faith and heirs of the kingdom. Then he adds, "But if you show partiality, you are committing sin and are convicted by the law as transgressors" (2:9).

Tragically, we frequently live as if God is running a mission only for the middle class. It's much easier to minister to people who can earn a respectable living, dress nicely on Sundays, and live in an acceptable home—preferably in a suburban neighborhood. It's always more difficult to relate to the poor, uneducated, and racially mixed groups. But such barriers were not a part of the ministry of Jesus. If the church is the salt of the earth, that salt must be found in all strata of society and among all ethnic communities.

In the book of Acts, the early church refused to associate with Gentiles. In order to rid them of such partiality, God had to use drastic measures. Peter was given a vision to coincide with an angel's visit to Cornelius (Acts 10:9–33). After he understood its significance, Peter risked his reputation to go to those dogs (an insulting term used for Gentiles), even though it was considered unlawful (v. 28). Gentiles can be grateful Peter persuaded his generation that the gospel was for them as well as the Jews. His words should be burned upon every heart and written in large letters on the outside of every church: "Truly I understand that God shows no partiality, but in every nation anyone who fears him and does what is right is acceptable to him" (Acts 10:34–35).

This concept is difficult to grasp. In a number of countries, children are starving, diseases are decimating the population, and war is ravaging the countryside. Is God really as interested in each of those children and adults as He is in us? Are the hairs of their heads numbered as well?

As Americans, it's easy to unconsciously assume that God has blessed us with more food than we can eat, more luxury than is good for us, and more money than any other country, simply because we are better or more important to the Almighty. Praying for our daily bread is out of the question. He gives us this day (and every day) our daily bread—and more.

Such feelings of superiority come under the same condemnation as the Pharisees received, who thanked God they were not like other men who deserved the fate that came upon them. But because they did not repent of their pride, they were excluded from God's program. And if God spared not the natural branches, what about us?

Furthermore, Jesus went out of His way to associate with people directly. The Pharisees criticized Him for eating with the tax collectors and sinners (Matthew 9:10). Jesus went to eat with Zacchaeus, a despised tax collector. All of this brought the wrath of the religious crowd upon Him. Jesus defended His actions by reminding them that He had come to seek and to save the lost, because those who were well didn't need a physician (Matthew 9:12). He also knew that the poor, the social outcasts, and those who had sinned greatly would be more responsive to His ministry. Having been forgiven much, they loved much. The religious elite didn't respond because they were righteous in themselves and didn't think they needed His help. Jesus therefore warned, "Truly, I say to you, the tax collectors and the prostitutes go into the kingdom of God before you" (Matthew 21:31). Such sinners didn't have to be rebuked for their sins; they were already conscious of the need for forgiveness.

This clarity of purpose and lack of hypocrisy should also be characteristic of us, His followers. Jesus did not tell sinners He loved them (at least, there is no such remark in the Gospels), but He demonstrated His concern by personal involvement. The people knew that He loved them; He did not have to say it.

Yet, when Jesus was in contact with the sinful society of His day, He remained uncontaminated. His sinlessness was not impaired because He ate and drank with sinners. Nor did His sinlessness prevent Him from association with sinners. There is no evidence that He cringed when He was in the company of evil men. He was able to love them, and they responded. But the religious leaders were different. Their hypocrisy and self-righteousness frequently stirred Jesus to anger and bitter denunciation.

What does this mean for us? Our separation from the world cannot be isolation from sinful society. The reverse is true. We, like Jesus, must associate with non-Christians so they will see our good works and glorify our Father who is in heaven (Matthew 5:16). And just as Christ revealed the Father by His life and teaching, we now have the same responsibility. The world should look at us and see the reflection of God. We are not deity as Jesus was, but as we submit to Jesus' life in us (the Spirit), His character (the fruit of the Spirit) is reproduced in us. God's program of truth being displayed in human form is still in effect. Except now, it is embodied in the lives of countless Christians who share the life of Christ and are part of His body on Earth—members of His flesh and bones (Ephesians 5:30).

Some say we cannot follow the example of Jesus in associating with sinners. He was incapable of sinning, but we are liable to succumb to temptation. Undoubtedly, any contact we have with the world involves some risk. Christ has not called us to safe living. We are as sheep in the midst of wolves. God does, however, require that we live righteously in the midst of a sinful, wicked, and adulterous generation. In fact, our ability to remain pure in the middle of a virtual Sodom and Gomorrah becomes the basis for proving the power of Christ to the world. History has shown that Christianity made a great impact on the Roman world because Christian families resisted the pressure of the sensual paganism of the day. The ultimate test for Christianity is purity within the pressure cooker of a sinful society, not isolation from it.

God called Abraham from Ur to live in Canaan, which separated him from his family but not from sinful influences. Canaan was extremely wicked, as archaeological exploration has shown. Every conceivable form of moral perversion was rampant. Whether Abraham could live a pure life in such a place was the test of his devotion to God.

The fact that such surroundings are dangerous can be seen from the life of Lot. He was weighed on the scale of moral temptation and found wanting. His environment forced him to make the ultimate choice of whether he would serve God or pleasure. Even if he had been isolated from Egypt and Sodom, would it have changed his choice? His environment contributed to his sin, but in actuality, it brought out what already was in his heart. His choice of the best pastureland showed that even before moving to Sodom, he was hooked on the world.

We face a choice: Should we pessimistically retreat from sinful society, or should we optimistically penetrate it with a wholesome life and witness? Should we be discouraged by the slippery slide of moral relativism, or should we use it to prove that our love for Christ is greater than the enticement of the world? If we choose the latter (as I hope we will do), we will need supernatural resources to cope with the temptations which will most certainly plague us.

But a warning is necessary! We must not let sinful

surroundings lead us into sin. And since we are all susceptible to sin, there will be times when we will have to withdraw from people who would encourage us to follow their ways. We must influence them to turn to God; we cannot let them influence us to turn to the world. A boy who bought a canary decided to put it in the same cage as a sparrow, hoping that the sparrow would learn to sing like the canary. After three days, he shook his head and remarked, "The sparrow doesn't sound like the canary; the canary sounds just like the sparrow."

When a sinful society begins to influence us, it's time to separate ourselves from it. When we begin to compromise our standards and enjoy the pleasures of sin, we have already crossed the boundary and identified ourselves with the world.

## PERSONAL SEPARATION

I met a girl named Barb when she was twenty-five. Her expression was sullen and bitter. She nervously ran her fingers along the seam of her tattered coat as she told me her story. Six years before, she had begun working in a Christian coffeehouse in order to share the gospel with the youth culture in a needy section of the city. Unfortunately, she had underestimated both the power of sin and the extent of her own weakness. Barb became acquainted with a young man who visited the coffeehouse regularly.

She felt uneasy about the relationship but told herself she was simply interested in witnessing to him. Within three months, they were married. And then the troubles began.

Her husband was on drugs and eventually became a pusher. They traveled from city to city, spending the night in run-down motels along the way. Under the constant pressures of the trade, Barb began to take drugs too, and eventually ended up in a hospital. Her husband quickly deserted her and lived freely with a variety of other girls. Barb soon discovered she was pregnant.

Emotionally she could no longer cope with reality. The trauma of drugs and the nightmare of a wrecked marriage were too much to handle.

Here was a girl who had memorized Scripture in Sunday school, who had come to know Christ as her Savior, and had dedicated herself to reaching others. Yet now she was a mental wreck. In her words, "There's no way out for me; not even God can solve my problems." Her frantic parents have asked a thousand times, "How far should we go in trying to win the world?" A good question.

We can enjoy the company of non-Christians and share mutual interests, but often we must say a polite "no thanks" to their suggestions. Furthermore, we may have to withdraw from them completely if we sense they could lead us astray. To keep ourselves from such a fate, let us briefly consider the warnings from God's Word.

The Scriptures are filled with warnings about the danger of going the way of the crowd. Those who are weak in their faith or who find it difficult to resist the sinful pleasures of others should be especially careful in choosing their friends. Solomon warned, "My son, if sinners entice you, do not consent" (Proverbs 1:10). Then he spelled out the ruin that would come to those who join in the wickedness of sinners. Another warning reads, "Be not envious of evil men, nor desire to be with them, for their hearts devise violence, and their lips talk of trouble" (Proverbs 24:1–2). Paul gives the same advice in Ephesians 5:5–12. Scores of passages have similar warnings. Thousands of individuals (often young people) have ruined their lives because they didn't choose their friends wisely. Today they have a police record, the physical and mental effects of illegal drugs, or an unhappy marriage, simply because they became friends with the wrong people.

How do we reconcile this with the previous section where we observed that Jesus, who is our example, was friends with the tax collectors and prostitutes? The key lies in our *motives* for friendship and our basic *desires* that control us.

Let us talk about motives first. We ought to love people because each one is a unique creation of God. Everyone bears the stamp of the Creator. We should love people whether they eventually become believers or not.

Our reason for friendship should be to display God's love indiscriminately.

Incidentally, when we are invited to participate in activities we cannot approve of, we should be careful to explain we are declining because of the activity itself. We are not rejecting our friends; we are rejecting what they do. If misunderstandings develop, we might lose their friendship. Sometimes this might be inevitable, but whenever possible, we must maintain rapport so they will feel free to talk to us about their deepest needs.

Our desires must also be examined. Evil will always be tempting and, on the surface, exciting. And because we usually slip into sin so gradually we scarcely notice it until it's too late—that's the problem we must always keep at the forefront of our minds when examining our motives and desires.

Many people think they are capable of enjoying sinful pleasures and know when to quit. Undoubtedly, it is possible to stop short of overt acts of sin while entertaining sinful attitudes and desires. But few—perhaps no one— does that indefinitely.

A con artist arrested in Chicago operated like this. He would convince a prospective customer that shares were available in a highly selective company. One-hundred dollars was guaranteed to double within a month. The prospect would be convinced this was "the real deal" because of the sheer volume of information the con artist was able to produce. A month later, the crook would promptly hand $200 in cash to his customer.

Several weeks later, the con artist would meet again with his client. This time, $500 was guaranteed to become $1,000 in three months. And it did.

During these months, the client would develop respect and faith in his new friend. Wasn't his friend faithful to his word? Hadn't the scheme worked? Yes. No one can argue with success.

A few months later, the men would meet again. This time, the customer gave his "friend" $10,000 which was guaranteed to double within six months. And *that* was the last time they met.

It's easy to develop trust in our ability to cope with a few choice sins. For a while, the pleasures seem to be an adequate payment for our compromise with the world. But one day, we will discover that we have been taken; payments other than pleasure become due. Our trust in our ability to control sin was misplaced. We have been duped.

Think of Barb again. She knew she shouldn't marry a non-Christian. She also knew that the purpose of courtship is to discover whether a friendship should develop into marriage. She knew these things but thought she could enjoy her relationship without harmful effects. And she was right, but not for long! She had come to trust sin, believing it would pay her dividends. And it did, though not the kind she had imagined.

Seldom do we sin for cash; usually we sin on credit. The bills do not come in immediately, but they will come due. We can sin now, but we must pay later.

The point is this: If we become ensnared with the sin around us today, we should have withdrawn from it yesterday! Guidelines are needed to prevent us from enjoying pleasures and habits which are designed to lead us astray. This is particularly true when we become friends with those whose entire life is bent toward evil. Never underestimate the power of uninhibited desire.

We need Christian coffeehouses. We need to share the gospel in the sin centers of our world. But when someone is morally and spiritually weak, the answer is separation from friends and environments that could lead to ruin. This will not guarantee Christian conduct, but it will help. We cannot choose our relatives, but thank God, we can choose our friends.

There are always opportunities for every Christian to befriend unbelievers without the risk of falling into sin. Think of the widow next door who is lonely, the neighbors who would enjoy a barbeque, and the assistant at work who would enjoy a game of golf. In such informal surroundings, people become open to the possibility of having God come into their lives. Friendly words coupled with gracious works will unlock almost any heart. Christianity is true, even if no one ever sees the Christian life lived. But in practice, few would ever believe unless they see the life lived. And they do not see it lived just because we say good morning with a smile.

We can be thankful that the days of the medieval monastery are over. Physical separation hardly meets our biblical mandate to be the salt of the earth. Living in an evil society can serve a good purpose. The world can either sharpen our spiritual life or dull it, depending on how we hold the blade. As Vance Havner observed, you can't sharpen an axe on a cake of butter!

May God give us the wisdom to live in the world for the right purpose. Contact without contamination is a possibility only with divine help.

## QUESTIONS FOR DISCUSSION

1. Describe the philosophies of separation.

2. How did Jesus' philosophy of separation relate to people? What valuable lesson did Jesus teach through His association with people? What warning must we heed?

3. How far should we go in trying to win the world? Discuss the scriptural warning about going the way of the crowd.

4. What is the key to developing friendships?

ERWIN W. LUTZER

CHAPTER FOUR

# THOSE SHORTCUTS TO EVANGELISM

Scores of Christians have never experienced the satisfaction of introducing someone to Jesus Christ. The reason for this malady is easy to find, namely, that scores of Christians have never had either the courage or the ability (or both) to give an intelligent presentation of the Good News. And since people believe only when they hear the essential ideas of salvation, we should not be surprised that only a small minority of individuals are coming to know Christ for themselves.

One of the solutions to the problem is the utilization of mass media. If professionals are given the opportunity to share the gospel with millions on television, on the radio, and on the internet, maybe people can be converted despite the ineptitude of "average" Christians. Whether such shortcuts to evangelism are effective will be discussed later. For now, let us consider personal witnessing.

Why are so few believers able to share their faith

intelligently? One reason is that they misunderstand the purpose of the church. They believe the method of reaching unbelievers is by inviting them to church where a professional (the preacher) will lead them to Christ. A hundred and fifty years ago, this method was more successful than it is now. Today, unbelievers consider church largely irrelevant, and the Sunday services can't compare to the drama of their favorite show or the latest podcast from an internet celebrity. Consequently, the vast majority of people come to church only for Easter, perhaps for Christmas, and maybe Thanksgiving. And when they do, they prefer their own church to that of their religious neighbor.

## PERSONAL WITNESSING

But all is not lost. The difficulty of doing evangelism within the church has caused many evangelical leaders to recapture the biblical purpose of the church, which is to equip the believers to do the work of the ministry (Ephesians 4:11–13). Seminars for lay evangelism are offered all over the country, and Christians who have never witnessed before are experiencing the joy of sharing their faith. As a result, their neighbors and friends are understanding for the first time what faith in Christ means. The church is beginning to leave the cloister and become more effective in penetrating the world.

In the book of Acts, the apostles were noted for their

preaching which got results. Peter was an outstanding evangelist who persuaded people to believe on Christ. Paul also preached effectively to large crowds. This kind of evangelism is still effective today, but it should not be used to excuse us from personal witnessing. It was the common people who began the spread of the gospel in the first century, and if we want to witness the growth of Christianity, we will have to use the same approach today (Acts 8:1). There is no shortcut to evangelism. As effective as Billy Graham was, his crusades were not a substitute for personal witnessing.

As an example of personal witnessing, consider Christ's encounter with the woman of Samaria in John 4. We are impressed by the fact that Jesus didn't avoid those who were grossly immoral nor those who may have been on the lowest rung of the social ladder. This woman had had five husbands. She should have known better, but that didn't deter Jesus, who was anxious that she be forgiven. Some of us would like to call down fire from heaven to wipe out those who live in immorality. But as we noted, Jesus made a sharp distinction between a sinner and sin. This story illustrates that superbly.

Today, we hear many suggestions about how to open up conversations with our neighbors and peers at work or school. Questions are often memorized and later used to begin a conversation which will eventually lead to three or four points explaining the gospel. Surely this is needed, and every believer should be able to ask such questions tactfully. But take a look at Jesus.

He was casually seated on Jacob's well, and when the woman arrived, He said, "Give me a drink." This request conveyed a needed bit of information to this woman, namely, that this particular Jew was friendly. He didn't despise her because she was a Samaritan. She felt free to immediately ask Him a question: "How is it that you, a Jew, ask for a drink from me, a woman of Samaria?" (John 4:9). Since He was obliging to her, she felt open to speak to Him. This leads us to the first lesson in personal evangelism: We must be friendly if we want people to consider trusting our best Friend. If we are unfriendly, they will reject us and our message.

It is not enough to say we have given someone the Good News; we must share it in the right way. In fact, people seldom reveal their deepest needs to someone who monopolizes the conversation or who leaves the impression he's uneasy in their presence. We all have an outer shell which can't be cracked by a dogmatic, insensitive person who is more concerned about speaking his piece than he is in us as individuals. Family problems, doubts, and existential questions are reserved only for those with listening ears and sympathetic hearts.

Jesus also showed His dependence on this woman by asking her to do something for Him. He didn't consider

Himself too dignified to ask a favor. He didn't talk down to her, pointing His finger at her with an air of superiority. From her viewpoint, He was one needy human being asking another for help. Such humility invariably breaks down barriers; superiority erects them.

The cure is to learn humility by shedding our indignant self-righteous attitude. Then we won't feel superior; we will know we are saved not because we are more intelligent or live honorable lives, but because God chose to save us. Love and concern will be the outgrowth of such gratitude to God. Others will be attracted to the Christ who controls us.

In His opening words, Jesus talked about an area of common interest—water. Similarly, we must share the common experiences of life with those who are in need. We live in an unjust, unfair, and unfeeling world. There are so few who are willing to take the time and make the effort to help bear the burdens and concerns of others. Yet this is necessary if the world is to believe we are for real.

As we share how Christ has met our specific needs, how He has helped us bear our burdens and has healed our emotional wounds, we will find that others will identify with us. They will see that we're not phonies (pretending we've never had a difficulty in all our lives) but that we have found Someone who can help us work through the disappointments of life.

We could go on to discuss how Jesus aroused the

woman's curiosity and pointed out her sin, but our purpose is not to provide a complete discussion of these principles. It is merely to emphasize that winning the world to Christ means winning individuals. And that responsibility cannot be delegated to pastors, missionaries, and evangelists alone. It falls squarely on your shoulders and mine.

Let's remember that the Holy Spirit doesn't work in a vacuum. Many Christians pray for the unsaved as though they expect God to simply break into the lives of people out of nowhere. It is true that the Holy Spirit will convict the world of sin, righteousness, and judgment, but Jesus prefaced this promise by saying He would send the Holy Spirit to the disciples (John 16:7–8). In other words, the Holy Spirit would do the work of conviction through the people who received the Spirit. The Spirit works through people today; He uses the message of a Christian's life (Paul speaks of adorning the doctrine of God by our attitude in Titus 2:10), and more specifically, the Spirit drives home the verbal message of the gospel.

We must push this point even further. Some Christians have a burden for foreign countries. They give their money to missionaries, support their church budget, and phone their friends to advertise missionary conventions. But they don't know the names of their neighbors across the street. Nor are they interested. They feel safer this way because getting to know others—especially unbelievers—can put them in awkward situations. *What shall we say if we are invited to attend a show we believe to be inappropriate or share some drinks?* they wonder. Such situations are sticky, and we have to learn to handle them. If we don't, the neighbors across the street may never hear the gospel. If they have never believed, they are just as lost as those in the tribal villages of South America or the Buddhists who believe there is no God. Yet, it's hard for us to accept the fact that the mission field is right next door.

It's easy to rationalize and say we're not solely responsible for sharing the gospel with our neighbors. Haven't they heard it—or at least had a chance to—through some religious program on television, or a podcast, or video on the internet? Hasn't this nation already been thoroughly evangelized by the proliferation of religious television, radio, and internet programs? Perhaps there's a shortcut to evangelism. Perhaps the day of individual messengers sharing the Good News has given way to the day of mass media. Perhaps we have done our duty when we give money to missions or send a generous gift to an organization committed to sharing the gospel through a weekly podcast or YouTube video. Perhaps not.

## THE WORLD AND IT'S METHODS

I remember in the 70s when I read the book *Future Shock* by Alvin Toffler, he predicted that we are living at an unprecedented hour of history: We are in the middle of a massive knowledge explosion. And if Toffler's predictions are even only partially correct, we have seen only the tip of a giant iceberg. Television, computers, the internet, and faster-than-sound planes are only the beginning of more sensational methods of travel and communication. How right he was! Kids growing up today scarcely recognize the world I grew up in. To answer the question of how Christians should relate to these rapid changes would require another book the size of Toffler's own voluminous work! Here, I will comment briefly on my attitude toward only one segment of our technological era: mass media.

Many people think mass media as a method of communication is neutral, but it's actually weighted against us to be instantly addictive. It's the *content* that determines whether mass media can be used for good or evil. Certainly, Christians should use these methods and tools to spread the Good News. But there are some inherent dangers in such methods. One is that we have a tendency to rely on various media forms instead of personal involvement to share the gospel of Christ. When God wanted to communicate His most complete revelation to man, He didn't equip the world with amplifiers and speakers then beam His message to all the nations. Rather, He became incarnate so we could not merely hear the message but *see it lived*. Undoubtedly many have been converted through seeing the message of

Christ presented in some sector of mass media: television, websites, books, etc. But such conversions have often been disappointing. Without the personal friendship and nurture of individual Christians, the seed often falls on shallow ground. There is a response—but not for long. The sun comes up, and the sprouting plant withers and dies.

Mass communication can aid in personal evangelism and the development of Christians, but it cannot be a substitute for the world seeing the truth lived *through us*. It's easy to think our hands have been washed from the responsibility of sharing our faith personally because of the proliferation of Christian programs on television, radio, and the internet. But the largest percentage of those who watch or listen to such programs are already committed to Christ. Jesus said it would be through our good works (and not merely our good words) that men would see our light shine and glorify our Father in heaven.

There is another danger. To make the message interesting, relevant, and palatable to the world, the gospel is often diluted when it's prepared for popular consumption. Some Christian music groups are so concerned about being inoffensive that even believers can scarcely find a clear biblical message in the songs. Ditto for some Christian films.

Communication today is supposed to be indirect, thought-provoking, and above all, entertaining. Christians who try to equal the production of the world in these respects usually come off a poor second. This is understandable, since the gospel is not exactly entertaining, nor is it a message which people care to hear. Certainly we should be tactful, but sometimes we are so conscious of our need to keep up with the techniques of the world system (which usually appeals to the carnal and frivolous appetites of the masses), that the gospel message loses its impact. All that the people remember is that our presentation was not as exciting as last night's reality tv episode.

Even religious advertising pays only minimum dividends. One church spent hundreds of dollars on advertisements to publicize a special speaker. The result: Not one person who attended the meetings did so because of the advertising. There is a basic fact of human nature we can't forget, namely, advertising is only effective in proportion to the desire people already have to attend the publicized event. Exciting movies, intriguing plays, and sensual amusements can draw throngs from a tiny advertisement. But God isn't popular. And only a very few people hunger and thirst after righteousness. Furthermore, many people have a stereotyped or even negative view of Christianity. Perhaps they had an unfortunate experience in the past, or maybe they heard stories that frightened them, or they may be confused because of the many denominations and sects all claiming to possess the truth. In bewilderment, the average non-Christian is determined to avoid anything associated with God or religion. Yet that person is still someone for whom Christ died, and they will never come to know Christ unless some Christian shows them love, compassion, and concern.

This critique of mass media doesn't mean that using such means is either wrong or worthless. We should favor new and creative methods of communication since they aid in evangelism and the development of Christians. But often, Christians prefer these methods of evangelism simply because they are impersonal. After all, when a form of media is used, people can be evangelized without our getting to know people personally and entering into their struggles and helping them in their need.

Often evangelistic radio, television, and internet-based events and programs are used to compensate for the lack of witnessing in the inner city or other difficult areas in our nation. But the fact remains that such methods simply do not reach the people who need the message the most. Many people are so disillusioned with religion they will never believe in Christ unless the message comes to them wrapped in a body. As Paul told the Corinthians, they were a letter, known and read by all men (2 Corinthians 3:2). Mass media cannot be a substitute for presenting the gospel personally to those who have little prior interest in religious matters. Individual Christians are the salt of the earth.

You may have heard that men look for better methods,

but God looks for better men. But maybe we haven't heard it often enough. It hasn't sunk in. There have been all sorts of schemes to get the attention of millions with the intention of evangelizing them en masse. But with all of these technological feats, belief in Christ is not spreading as rapidly as in the first century when Christianity swept the Roman Empire.

We are responsible for telling our neighbors the Good News. And we will be effective to the extent that we have learned the secret the early Christians learned: Men and women who have received Christ have the power of the Holy Spirit to enable them to witness. "Not by might, nor by power, but by my Spirit, says the LORD of hosts" (Zechariah 4:6).

## QUESTIONS FOR DISCUSSION

1. Why are so few believers able to share their faith intelligently?

2. Read Ephesians 4:11–13. What do these verses mean to our evangelical mission today?

3. Discuss Jesus' encounter with the woman of Samaria. What lessons can we learn from Him that will help us further the gospel?

4. What should be the believer's attitude toward mass media?

CHAPTER FIVE

# TAKING YOUR SPIRITUAL TEMPERATURE

Christmas is a time of reunion, travel, gifts, and for many, loneliness. It's also a time for sermons. Since history repeats itself with uncanny regularity, someone inevitably preaches a sermon about the innkeeper at Bethlehem. That unnamed man of two thousand years ago is often derided, judged, and condemned. By implication, he is classified along with Judas and a few other ignoble souls who put their scar on the history of mankind. Specifically, he is faulted for forcing the Messiah to be born in a stable.

Before we consign the innkeeper to the company of reprobates, let us rethink the situation. Remember, he didn't know Mary was going to give birth to the Son of God. He thought Mary and Joseph were just a young Jewish couple who had the misfortune of arriving after all of the rooms were taken. Yes, Mary was pregnant, but he didn't know when she would give birth. Furthermore, his inn was full. Imagine asking people in a hotel to give up their rooms, even to a pregnant woman. He couldn't accommodate this couple, even though he probably wished he could.

If he had known that Mary bore the Son of God, he likely would have found a place for them. There is always room for one or two more, especially for the Creator Himself. Or so it would seem.

Let's suppose we had the privilege of inviting Christ into our homes. Would we accept the opportunity? If He needed clothes, would we give Him some? If so, would we give Him the best? Or the worst? The answer to these questions is not as obvious as it might seem. Many Christians evidently wouldn't visit Him in prison if He were sick, nor would they feed Him if He were hungry, nor would they give Him clothes if He were dressed in rags.

Jesus taught that we do have the opportunity to help Him in these ways today. The innkeeper at Bethlehem innocently refused to make room for Christ, today we can refuse Him deliberately. And we do.

When have we overlooked Christ's needs? When did we have a chance to help Him but didn't? Jesus predicted those questions would be asked by some people in the future, so He answered it Himself: "For I was hungry and you gave me *no food*, I was thirsty and you gave me *no drink*, I was a stranger and you *did not welcome me*, naked and you *did not clothe me*" (Matthew 25:42–43, italics added). Then Christ explains, "Truly, I say to you, as you did not do it to one of the least of these, you did not do it to me" (v. 45). Even a cup of cold water given in His name will not go unnoticed by the Father (Matthew 10:42).

In the Scriptures, hospitality is one of the key marks of Christian love; snobbish cliques are an evidence of carnality and worldliness. For example, when James defined true religion, he did not say it was church attendance or the ability to teach (although he would have favored such activities), rather, he defined it as visiting orphans and widows in their distress (James 1:27). Putting a twenty dollar bill in the offering plate once or twice a month for the needs of the less fortunate is not difficult. That's only a minor inconvenience; parting with twenty dollars is painful, but not for long. Hospitality means more than these things; it requires personal involvement. It takes time, patience, and is often inconvenient. That's why it's one of the most accurate indicators of our spiritual pulse.

Of course, worldly Christians—and even non-Christians—can practice hospitality. Natural human concern cares for others. But Christianity demands a level of caring that transcends human inclinations. Christian hospitality has a supernatural quality distinguishing it from the Red Cross, Welcome Wagon, and other public organizations. It even differs from the usual custom of having our best friends join us for Thanksgiving. Hospitality, *Christian* hospitality, goes beyond ordinary human good.

Suppose you want someone to enjoy a meal with you. Or maybe you would like to have people over for coffee after church on Sunday. Whom shall you invite? Your answer could reflect your spiritual temperature. If we invite only those who admire us, if we invite only those who are on the same social level or one level higher, we may be motivated by purely human love.

Jesus taught that if we love those who love us, we will have no reward, for even the tax collectors do the same (Matthew 5:46). So, what are the elements of *Christian* hospitality?

## WHAT CHRISTIAN HOSPITALITY IS NOT

Jesus said, "When you give a dinner or a banquet, do not invite your friends or your brothers or your relatives or rich neighbors" (Luke 14:12). He didn't mean we should never have our relatives or friends in our home; the implication is that this should not become a habit. It's easy to fall into the rut of having one relative invite another and then switch homes the next week. Or consider church cliques where members invite only those who are within their circle of friends. Church members may find it easy to be friendly to everyone within the innocuous confines of the church building, yet at the same time, they may reserve the deepest level of friendship for a select few. The tragedy is that many—sometimes the most needy—are bypassed when the invitations are passed out.

Others may cater to the rich in order to make an impression, hoping the rich will invite them in return. James uses a similar situation as a classical illustration of worldliness. In the first century, rings were a status symbol, much like new cars are today. Those who entered the church wearing such expensive jewelry were greeted warmly and given a place of honor. The church members took special pains to make the rich feel welcome. On the other hand, a poor man was greeted with indifference. The church didn't reject him; the members just didn't really care if he attended or not. Nor were they concerned about his needs. James says that such partiality is sin (James 2:1–13).

Whenever we accept people because of their money, we have capitulated to worldly values. Wealth doesn't influence God; if it does with us, we have strayed from His viewpoint. God values spiritual assets more than financial; when we reverse the two, we are friends with the world and are therefore displaying hostility toward God. In fact, James says the rich are often the ones who oppress the needy and squeeze the last dime from the poor. To court the rich and despise the poor is to be married to the world.

Hospitality, like friendliness, should be displayed indiscriminately. The path of least resistance is to like the likable, be friends with the rich, and become a part of a clique. Civic groups and neighborhood celebrations are often built on such relationships.

God calls us to a higher level of concern. He commands us to love our neighbor as ourself; to do good to all men, particularly to those who are of the household of faith. That requires more than visiting with the "prominent" families in the church, who already have more social engagements than they can manage. God's call goes beyond the present to the future; it is heavenly rather than earthly; it runs contrary to human values and inclinations.

## WHAT CHRISTIAN HOSPITALITY IS

Whom shall we befriend? James wrote that pure religion (outward expression of inward faith) is to visit the orphans and the widows (1:27). This phrase was used in the Old Testament to refer to anyone who had a need and could not repay the favor. Jesus put it this way, "But when you give a feast, invite the poor, the crippled, the lame, the blind, and you will be blessed, because they cannot repay you. For you will be repaid at the resurrection of the just" (Luke 14:13–14). Whom shall we invite? Those who come to church in work clothes. Then we should look for those who cause us some inconvenience (the crippled, the lame, and the blind).

The poor may never compliment us for the decor of our living rooms nor ask about the paintings on the wall. The blind may never tell us how beautiful our furniture looks. Yet these are the ones we are to befriend. One thing is certain: Christian hospitality is not motivated by self-interest, for if we take Christ's advice, we won't be repaid for our efforts, at least not now. Christian hospitality means helping those who could never pick up the tab.

Christ's instructions are difficult to obey. Getting acquainted with strangers isn't easy. For some people, it seems impossible. We feel more at home with those who know our preferences and have enough insight to appreciate us. Strangers often tax our patience, talk about trivial matters, and don't laugh at our jokes. To avoid such a painful experience, we are tempted to invite our favorite friends for another rerun of previous social contracts. And we call it hospitality.

Jesus said those who exercised true hospitality would be rewarded at the resurrection of the just. What He did not mention is that there are special blessings for us even now if we follow His advice. When we make an effort to get to know strangers, we'll soon discover we are enriched by their friendship. Abraham showed hospitality to strangers and later discovered he had entertained angels without knowing it. Later, this episode is used in Hebrews 13:1–2 to encourage hospitality. Much to our surprise, we will be blessed by those whom we never dreamed would become our friends. We will appreciate the words of Jesus: "It is more blessed to give than to receive" (Acts 20:35).

## PERSONAL INVOLVEMENT

All of us have a natural inclination to hide our true self from others. We may be lonely, defeated, and discouraged, yet we give an impression of confidence, optimism, and even joy. Barriers build up over a period of many years and cannot easily be torn down. Sometimes we think other people would reject us if we acted and talked the way we really felt. More likely, we would discover that our honesty would be refreshing to them, so refreshing that they in turn would be honest with us. Yet such levels of friendship do not usually happen by accident.

In fact, it's probable that we don't know the anxieties of our best friends. When we're with them, we simply talk about the events of the day or our plans for the future. Family problems, doubts, and frustrations may be driving them to despair and we might be unaware of it.

For that matter, we can show hospitality and still not meet someone's deepest need. Even the poor may have problems deeper than hunger; the defeated may have struggles beyond the usual temptations. How then shall we bear one another's burdens and so fulfill the law of Christ (Galatians 6:2)?

The answer lies in establishing levels of friendship beyond the usual pleasantries. Specifically, it means developing the most important of all Christian virtues: love. Some Christians are discouraged because they have few gifts or feel inadequate. Yet love is higher than the other gifts in value; love is the one gift open to every member of the church.

Love is not dependent on ability, popularity, or shrewdness. The greatest path is open to the least of travelers.

Without love, oratory is worth nothing. Even the ability to move mountains by prayer or the ultimate sacrifice of martyrdom is worthless unless done with love. Love doesn't seek vindication; nor does it tolerate bitterness. It controls our tongues because it always believes the best, hopes the best, and endures everything. Love accepts people as they are; love can take insults without ill will.

Little wonder Paul says love will remain after all the other gifts are gone (see 1 Corinthians 13). After sermons have been forgotten, after Christian organizations have folded, and our records are outdated, only love will abide.

Why does the Scripture zero in on love as the greatest virtue? One reason is that it runs contrary to the fiber of human nature. Left by ourselves, we take care only of interests that help us. We show concern only when it's appreciated; we love those who love us. Or we love those who can be loved without inconvenience.

Hospitality is a test for godliness because those who are selfish don't like strangers (especially needy ones) to intrude upon their private lives. They prefer their own friends who share their lifestyle. Only the humble have the necessary resources to give of themselves to those who could never give of themselves in return.

Hospitality also means work. A dinner is not the

product of an accident, as every cook is quick to confess. Yet it is in such informal friendships that the true needs and cares of others are revealed. This can be the beginning of more extended concern.

Since love is opposed to our sinful world, it is here that we have the best opportunity to demonstrate supernatural ability. Love defined in the Scriptures goes beyond the boundaries of human concern, and for that very reason, it is the gift of God.

On a trip to Dallas, I stopped at a restaurant in Missouri. A conversation opened with the waitress; she openly shared her guilt and domestic problems. Twenty-five minutes later, she prayed to receive Christ as her Savior. During the discussion, she said to me, "I used to attend a church, but they didn't care about us: we weren't part of the group. And we couldn't afford the clothes they had, so we weren't accepted. Why does a church exist if it doesn't love people?" An excellent question. Why does it?

The opportunity the innkeeper in Bethlehem had is ours today. Christ can be invited to our home and enjoy His favorite meal. He can sleep in our bed, and we can quench His thirst. "Truly, I say to you, as you did it to one of the least of these my brothers, you did it to me" (Matthew 25:40).

How is your spiritual temperature?

## QUESTIONS FOR DISCUSSION

1. Read Matthew 25:42–43. How may these verses be applied to Christians today?
2. Why is hospitality one of the key marks of Christian love?
3. Describe the elements of Christian hospitality.
4. Read James 2:1–13. Why is such partiality sin?
5. When is hospitality not enough? What must we do to meet the deeper needs of others?

ERWIN W. LUTZER

CHAPTER SIX

# RESOLVING OUR DIFFERENCES

What happens when your opinion about conduct collides with that of another Christian? Should you go to a different church? Resolve the dispute by discussion? Or tell them to mind their own business?

For example, I know a man who was converted at the age of twenty-five. Before that, he had spent long hours gambling and playing pool at a local tavern.

When he trusted Christ as his Savior, the first major adjustment was to abandon the game he had come to love. With his new set of priorities, he had no time for pool, which had ensnared him these many years.

Sometime later, he was invited to a Christian home for dinner. To pass time, his Christian friend suggested they have a game of pool. The new convert was appalled. He couldn't believe any Christian could play such a sinful game. Yet his friend insisted that pool was as innocent as ping-pong or shuffleboard.

Often we have the liberty to enjoy an activity another Christian considers wrong. We might be tempted to go ahead with what we have planned on the grounds that we alone are accountable to God for our own actions. Why should we not enjoy our liberty just because someone else seems offended?

Churches have often been divided over rather petty issues some believers consider crucial. One group is convinced a certain sport is harmless; others believe it's a compromise with the world. So even though our own conscience may be clear, we can't do whatever we wish. The Scriptures teach that we have to take other Christians into account. Both the churches at Corinth and Rome had to have instructions about how to handle sensitive questions.

A word of caution is in order. When Paul gave instructions to the churches at Corinth and Rome regarding personal liberty, he was speaking about issues which, in themselves, were morally neutral. By "morally neutral," I simply mean that the activity per se was not sinful. Eating meat offered to idols or living according to the dietary laws of the Old Testament was not intrinsically sinful; these practices became sin if they were done legalistically or if they hindered the spiritual growth of others.

Sometimes 1 Corinthians 8 and Romans 14 are used as a basis to discuss activities such as those which will be discussed later, questionable amusements, and harmful habits. But these activities should not be automatically classified as "neutral" without any further ado. Although we might disagree on some of the specifics, the usual list of sins associated with worldliness does have important moral implications. Certain principles of Scripture remove some activities from the neutral category and place them in the forbidden column. Obviously, when Paul talks about the Christian's liberty to eat meat or not to eat it, he is referring to a matter which, of itself, is not designed to appeal to our carnal nature. It is not sin of itself.

The ancient city of Corinth was a center of paganism and sexual permissiveness. Part of the pagan worship involved offering meat to the gods. The priest would take the meat presented by the worshiper and put it upon the altar. Shortly afterward, the meat was taken to the marketplace and sold for less than a comparable cut which had come directly from the slaughterhouse. When the pagans became Christians, they soon realized that idols were nothing, therefore the meat offered to them was not polluted in any way. And so they freely bought the meat without any qualms. But there were other Christians, weak in the faith. They remembered having worshiped some of those pagan gods and felt that if they ate the meat which had been offered to those supposed deities, this would entangle them in their past idolatry. This group would buy the more expensive cuts lest they defile their conscience by eating meat which had been offered to idols.

The church almost split on this issue. One Christian would accuse another of narrow-mindedness: after all, an idol was nothing, so why should one's conscience be defiled by eating meat offered to it? But the other Christians would say that such reasoning approves of association with idols and does not represent true separation from the world.[1]

How can such a dispute be resolved? Paul begins by saying a Christian is not always free to exercise his liberty simply because he has knowledge (the understanding that an idol is nothing). Simply because some believers knew they *could* eat meat did not mean they *should* eat it. Admittedly, God has declared all foods clean, so believers should not become entangled by imposing a law upon themselves. But Christians should be willing to curb their freedom if it helps a weaker Christian. Paul says there are some who don't have knowledge; they consider eating meat offered to idols as a concession to paganism. And so he warns, "But take care that this right of yours does not somehow become a stumbling block to the weak" (1 Corinthians 8:9).

Remember the man who was a slave to the game of pool before he was converted? He didn't have the knowledge (at that time) to see that pool is no different from any other games in principle. But because he had been a slave to it, he falsely assumed the game was wrong for every Christian.

What does the Scripture say to this situation? To God

it makes no difference: a pool table is nothing. But just because believers are free to play pool, that doesn't mean they *ought* to do so. They should be willing to restrict their liberty by refraining to play lest they be a stumbling block to the weaker believer. Furthermore, Paul writes that if our liberty causes the believer to be ruined, then by "sinning against your brothers and wounding their conscience when it is weak, you sin against Christ" (1 Corinthians 8:12). To knowingly wound the conscience of a fellow believer (even if that conscience be misguided) is to sin against Christ Himself.

Unfortunately, this principle has often been misinterpreted. Some have felt that anything a Christian does which another dislikes means the Christian is being a stumbling block. Not necessarily. Jesus frequently said and did things that caused offense—even for His own disciples. If He had been concerned about offending the Pharisees, He most assuredly would not have healed people on the Sabbath. Nor would He have eaten with the tax collectors and sinners. After all, these actions offended the religious elites beyond measure.

Consider another example. A seminary professor whose hobby was driving sports cars was told by one of his students, "Your new car is a stumbling block to me." But this is a misuse of this biblical principle. The car was not a stumbling block; the student was probably envious of the new model, especially when he compared it to his own collection of nuts and bolts. If the term *stumbling block* is not correctly defined, it's obvious that we might well find we can do nothing at all: Christians can take offense or be hurt by almost anything because of envy. You are not a stumbling block simply because you do something which others do not like or of which they disapprove.

What then does it mean to be a stumbling block or to wound the conscience of a weaker believer? Paul uses it to refer to any actions or words which would *make them fall back into their former way of life*. In Romans, Paul broadens this definition somewhat, although the basic meaning remains the same. The one who ate meat offered to idols may feel this is associated with the paganism of the past; the one who played pool may be led back to his former life of vulgarity and gambling; the one whose god was sports may be tempted to worship that god again if he is expected to participate. One Christian who has freedom in these matters might find he should surrender his liberty for the benefit of another whose weak conscience can be easily defiled. The weak believer feels convicted because he believes he is returning to the mire from which he was rescued.

In summary, we can say that what is safe for one person may not be safe for another. We may resist a temptation that is too great for someone else and, conversely, we may err in matters where they are strong. Therefore, nothing should be judged merely from the standpoint of knowledge but rather from the motivation of love. We must not only ask what we can do but rather what we *should* do for the benefit of other believers. A pleasure that isn't harmful for us but which may contribute to the ruination of someone else is not a legitimate pleasure but a sin. And that sin is not merely against our fellow believer but against the Lord Himself.

## THE PROBLEM AT ROME

In Romans 14:1–15:3, Paul is even more specific regarding Christian liberty. He gives four timeless principles that should be the hallmark of all godly living. Some of the Christians in Rome had a Jewish heritage, while others were converted out of paganism. Problems were bound to develop. For example, some of the Jews were still convinced that the dietary laws of the Old Testament should be kept; others accepted the new revelation that such requirements were a thing of the past (Acts 10). Here, as in 1 Corinthians, Paul emphasizes that love and harmony should exist in the church. Then he gives principles to resolve the disagreement.

First, the weak believer should not judge the strong and vice versa. Those who understood God's new revelation of freedom from the dietary laws of the Old Testament (those who were strong), were not to judge those who didn't feel free to eat meat (the weak).

Parenthetically, let's remember that Paul taught that

those believers who had liberty were the strong, while those who didn't have the freedom to eat meat were the weak believers. Today, Paul's teaching is often perverted to mean something else. Many Christians tacitly assume that the Christian who has liberty to enjoy certain activities is weak, while the one who is strong realizes such freedom is a capitulation to the world. Paul taught the opposite. A strong Christian will see that morally-neutral activities should not be forbidden categorically. A weak Christian who doesn't understand liberty in Christ will often want to multiply taboos, still thinking that spiritual living is conforming to the right set of "don'ts." In Rome, the strong Christian could eat meat with a clear conscience; the weak Christian could not.

However, it's important that *neither* the weak nor the strong should judge each other. If a person considers himself strong, he will not judge someone who is weak.

Often we hear such remarks as, "They are so legalistic they wouldn't even go to a Christian film when it's shown in a theater." Such snobbishness is sin. The believer may have such convictions without necessarily being legalistic. Yet, by the same token, the one who is not free to go to such an event should not judge those who do. The strong Christian who sees that the theater in and of itself is nothing, should not judge the weaker Christian who believes their own presence there would be a compromise with the world.

Paul says God has received both.

Let us suppose you, along with a number of others, were servants in a household. Would it be your responsibility to judge the performance of one of your peers? No. Paul says, "Who are you to pass judgment on the servant of another? It is before his own master that he stands or falls" (Romans 14:4). Paul uses the illustration of the Sabbath to prove his point. After the Jews were saved, they could not break the habit of observing the seventh day of the week rather than the first (Sunday). What was Paul's response? "One person esteems one day as better than another, while another esteems all days alike. Each one should be fully convinced in his own mind" (v. 5). If both acknowledge Christ as Lord, the day itself is not that important; rather, we must realize our attitude is what counts. If both believers acknowledge Christ as Lord and are fully aware they shall individually give account of themselves to God, then we should not be so quick to judge (vv. 11–12).

This problem of liberty raises the question of Sunday activities such as sports. With the advent of the television set (and subsequent technologies), we no longer have to leave our house to view athletic games on Sunday. If we say it's acceptable to watch but sin to attend or participate, we'll soon be caught in a host of hair-splitting distinctions. Perhaps there's room for individual differences. It is conceivable that the Master may permit one person to be involved, whereas another should refrain from even watching sports on Sunday. At any rate, let's be careful not to judge unless some other spiritual principle is violated in the sports craze on Sunday afternoons.

The previous paragraphs should not be interpreted to mean we should not consider Sunday as a special day of worship. Even though it's not a continuation of the Sabbath, it does perpetrate the principle that one day in seven should be set aside for rest and worship. Furthermore, Christians should honor God with their money on that day (1 Corinthians 16:1–2); and above all, it's a commemoration of Christ's resurrection. With a great number of events now scheduled on Sundays, we might well decide to shun them all in order to worship God without interruption. Any competition for our time always forces us to choose for God or for ourselves. But since there are no specific commands given to tell us what should *not* be done on the first day of the week, we should recognize that we cannot impose our own rules on another believer. Before their own Master, they stand or fall.

Second, Paul says that the liberty of one fellow believer should not be exercised if it causes another to stumble (Romans 14:13). We have already considered this in discussing 1 Corinthians 8. But here Paul uses three expressions to describe what might happen to weak believers if we don't consider them in our actions. The weak believers might stumble (fall back into sin) or be offended (question and discredit our testimony), and they could be weakened (revert to legalism simply to defend their position against what they would consider moral license).

Rather than let this happen, Paul says we should pursue the things which make for peace and the edification of one another. The unity of the church and the strengthening of other Christians should override our desire to exercise our liberty. Therefore, it's good not to eat meat or drink wine or do anything which causes our fellow Christian to stumble.

Earlier we noted that being offended means one is tempted to go back to their former way of life. Perhaps these three expressions—*stumble, be offended,* and *weakened*—here could be summarized by saying we shouldn't do anything that would hinder the spiritual growth of someone else or cause them to doubt the reality of their conversion experience. But as we said before, this doesn't mean we must refrain from anything other Christians might happen to dislike. Rather, we should refrain from those activities that impair our fellow believer's *spiritual* welfare.

Third, Paul stressed the need of having a clear conscience (Romans 14:22–23). This principle applies equally to the weak and the strong. The weak Christian should not do anything they cannot do in faith, even if it is a harmless activity. If they eat meat, which is technically legitimate, but does so with a feeling of self-condemnation and without conscious dependence on God, then it is sin. If they cannot bring themselves to believe God's declaration that the law no longer applies, they are doubting God's approval on their conduct and "whatever does not proceed from faith is sin" (v. 23).

Since the conscience is often tempered by environment, some people may feel convicted when doing the most trivial actions. Within time, they may begin to accept God's revelation regarding Christian liberty; until that happens, they are sinning if they cannot do these activities in good conscience. Let us remember that the strong Christian cannot have a clear conscience even if they do what is legitimate for them, if at the same time their conduct impairs the spiritual life of a fellow believer. And the strong believer should realize that they have the primary responsibility. "We who are strong have an obligation to bear with the failings of the weak, and not to please ourselves" (Romans 15:1).

Finally, Paul says that rather than pleasing ourselves, we should do all to glorify God (Romans 15:6). A widespread notion making the rounds teaches that when we curb our liberty, we are automatically putting ourselves under legal bondage. Since we are to enjoy our liberty in Christ, some think we are legalistic if we don't do everything we may have the right to do. But Paul clearly taught that one could have Christian liberty without exercising it. And for this reason, we should gladly conform to certain disciplines rather than hinder our fellow believer's spiritual welfare. The strong Christian retains their liberty though they do not use it. If, because of selfishness, a believer insists that they should do whatever they feel they are at liberty to do, they are unlike Christ who did not please Himself (Romans 15:3). Jesus did not do merely that which was convenient for Himself, rather, He acted for our good.

If we judge our conduct by Jesus and His desire to please the Father, we will solve many decisions regarding behavior. Will my actions attract individuals to Christ? Will it cause them to use my actions as license for their misuse of liberty? And finally, am I causing division in the church because of my misuse of liberty?

These questions are necessary in exercising our freedom among other believers. Strong Christians should be the first to adjust their liberty accordingly. If playing a certain game or engaging in a certain activity causes our fellow Christian to stumble, we should be willing to curb our liberty for their good. Paul would have done that, and so should we.

## QUESTIONS FOR DISCUSSION

1. What do we mean when we speak of a "morally neutral" issue?

2. Read 1 Corinthians 8–9. When are we free to exercise Christian liberty? When should we not?

3. Read Romans 14:1–15:3. What four principles regarding Christian liberty may we extract from this passage? In what way may we use those principles?

# PART II

# ANALYZING THE WORLD SYSTEM

ERWIN W. LUTZER

CHAPTER SEVEN

# THOSE DON'TS AND DOS

"Many of the students here look at the world and think they have been given the short end of the stick," remarked a coed at one of our leading Christian schools. "They envy those who are enjoying sinful pleasures." She spoke more profoundly than she knew. Many Christians resent their spiritual heritage, because they believe life would be more fun if they had no restrictions cramping their lifestyle. They're convinced that by trusting Christ as their Savior, they've gained very little—at least in this life. Maybe it will pay off in the wild blue yonder, but for the here and now, it's a disappointment. They've been tricked.

Satan got Eve to believe a similar story in the Garden of Eden. He got her to concentrate on the one negative (the forbidden tree) so she'd be distracted from the positive blessings (the many trees from which she could eat). In one master stroke of genius, he was able to convince her that God was withholding something good. If she would only disobey God's command, she would then be like Him, knowing good from evil.

Eve believed Satan's lie. God was indeed withholding something good from her. She looked with envy at the fruit of the forbidden tree. Surely this restriction was not for her benefit. God had given this command because He didn't want her to enjoy life to the fullest. He just wanted to keep her under His thumb. And so she ate the fruit. But nothing turned out quite like Eve had imagined. The fruit tasted good, but as a result of the disobedience, a host of problems appeared. And it all began when Eve thought being restricted from one tree meant she was receiving the short end of the stick.

There is a fable of a kite which once said to itself, "If I could just get rid of that man who is holding me back, then I could fly above the clouds and kiss the stars." One day the string broke. Now at last, it was free to soar higher than it had ever gone before. But much to its surprise, it didn't rise. In fact, it came crashing down to the ground. The kite hadn't realized a fact of aerodynamics: the string holding a kite down is the string holding it up. A kite can fly above the clouds only when the man on Earth is in full control.

God's restrictions not only hold us down but they also hold us up. We will never achieve fulfillment unless He is in full control. He didn't send His Son to cramp our lifestyle but to give us a much better one. And if we're not finding that to be true, something drastic has gone wrong.

But how do we go about deciding which actions are right or wrong? How do we solve those sticky questions regarding amusements, habits, and lifestyles?

Some acts are always sin regardless of the circumstances. It's always wrong to break the commandments which have been expressly revealed. For example, adultery, lying, and stealing are always sin and cannot be justified by the situation. Then there are numerous negative commands in the New Testament. It's always sin to be conformed to the world (Romans 12:2), to permit unwholesome words to proceed out of our mouths (Ephesians 4:29), to grieve the Holy Spirit (Ephesians 4:30), or to be ashamed of the testimony of the Lord (2 Timothy 1:8). Living under grace does not mean we are free from following the commands in God's Word.

Then there are some things that are always right. For example, it's always proper to love one another (Romans 12:10), to set our minds on things above rather than things on Earth (Colossians 3:2), to let the peace of Christ rule in our hearts (Colossians 3:15), and to give thanks in every circumstance (1 Thessalonians 5:18). This list could be expanded almost indefinitely. There are scores of such exhortations in the New Testament which are the will of God for us all.

But the fact is there are many questionable activities

which are difficult to classify categorically as "sinful" or "not sinful." What about movies, video games, social media, Sunday sports, television, the internet, or social drinking? Is it possible for Christians to engage in or utilize these things without being worldly? Or should such a list be used to define precisely what worldliness is?

One Christian, who had become weary of the disagreements regarding the specifics of Christian conduct, made this suggestion: A group of church leaders ought to form a list of sinful activities so the average Christian could know at a glance what is sin and what is not. Then we could just follow the list rather than constantly face such decisions on our own.

On the surface, this suggestion might seem feasible or at least worth a try. But a closer analysis will show that such an assignment can never be done. It sounds simple, but in practice, it's impossible.

Even if we made a complete list of all the commands of Scripture, we could not thereby solve all of the problems associated with Christian conduct. For one thing, even innocent actions can *become* sin if we are inordinately attached to them; for another, our different weaknesses make it impossible to specify appropriate conduct for everyone.

Disagreements on these matters force us to examine the basis of our conduct. We must understand why opinions have been divided on these and similar issues. Let us begin by clarifying the misused and misunderstood word, *legalism.*

## THE MEANING OF LEGALISM

A Christian who lives according to certain standards and in harmony with a list of commandments is often classified as a legalist. Advocates of the new morality give the erroneous impression that the very existence of laws or rules results in legalistic behavior. But in the Old Testament, God spelled out His will in the Ten Commandments and hundreds of other detailed laws (613 to be exact). If the very existence of laws constitute legalism, then God has obviously encouraged legalism in every conceivable form. However, obedience to laws does not constitute legalism. A Christian who lives within the commands of the New Testament—or even regulations he has set up for himself— is not necessarily legalistic. He may be—but not necessarily.

What then is legalism? It is a *wrong use* of laws and rules. Or, to put it another way, legalism results by ascribing the wrong function to the Law. Basically, three forms of legalism are referred to in the Scripture. First, there is the legalism of those who believed salvation could be attained by keeping the Law. For example, the rich young ruler thought he had kept the Law from his youth; such obedience was commonly believed to be sufficient for salvation.

Literally millions living today have a similar view. They think that God has a scale in heaven, and if their good works and deeds outweigh the bad, they will be received with the righteous in the day of judgment. "If I do my best and try to live up to the Sermon on the Mount, what else can God expect?" they ask impatiently. They don't realize that God demands infinitely more, so much so that only those clothed in the righteousness of Christ receive His approval. Legalism is the belief that keeping moral laws (or attempts to) will correct a man's relationship with God.

Second, there is the legalism of the Jews mentioned in Galatians who believed that although salvation was free and to be accepted by faith, living the Christian life (walking in the Spirit) was a simple matter of keeping the Law. Having begun in the Spirit, they now hoped to be made mature by works of the flesh (Galatians 3:1–3). This sort of legalism is frequently found in evangelical circles, where the gospel is clearly presented, then the saved are asked to conform to certain patterns of behavior to become mature in Christ. Of course, if there is immoral conduct, new converts should be exhorted to bring their conduct in line with biblical requirements. However, as we shall see later, even this does not *produce* spirituality.

Third, there is the legalism of the Pharisees who not only tried to keep the Law for personal salvation but also went beyond the teachings of Scripture by adding their own customs to the Old Testament Law. For example, the Mosaic law forbade the practice of reaping on the Sabbath (Exodus 34:21). But it did permit a hungry traveler to pluck and eat corn from another's field so long as he used his hands and not a sickle (Deuteronomy 23:25). But the Pharisees felt that plucking corn on the Sabbath came close to reaping, and in order to be sure everyone stayed well within the prescribed limits, they felt that merely eating corn while walking through a field on the Sabbath should be regarded as sin too. Christ did not adhere to such additions to the Law and accused them of teaching the traditions of men as the commandments of God (Mark 7:7).

This type of legalism is still popular today. Christians often go beyond scriptural teaching in defining what Christian conduct involves. Sometimes this is done because biblical principles are thought to be at stake; at other times, rules are made which confuse cultural mores (customs attached to a given country or locality) with biblical teachings. For example, hairstyles and dress codes are sometimes the yardstick used to measure worldliness. Of course there are those who dress immodestly and others who are slaves to fashions. But many of our accepted standards are merely conventional. In some churches, the men who serve the elements on communion Sunday are required to wear white shirts for the meeting. Lower standards (colored shirts) are apparently fine for less spiritual occasions. This shows what happens when we confuse biblical principles with social conventions.

We could clarify such confusion by listing the traditions of churches and then giving the chapter and verse upon which these traditions are based. After that, we could evaluate our practices in order of their importance. For example, Christ told the Pharisees they had done right in tithing but they had neglected the weightier matters of the Law, such as justice, mercy, and faithfulness (Matthew 23:23). He also said that what went into a man (the outward) was not as important as what proceeded from with his heart (Mark 7:18–23). This assignment would help us see the essential in contrast to the peripheral. We would discover that we're not really becoming worldly merely because some men are growing beards and others are wearing colored shirts.

What about instances where moral principles *are* involved? Is it not logical to specify precisely what amusements, habits, and vocations are acceptable and which ones are not? This question will be discussed in detail later. For now, it's sufficient to note that the legalism of the Pharisees was not only the error of thinking that the keeping of the Law was all God demanded, but they also added to its requirements in their quest for righteousness.

To summarize, legalism is a misunderstanding of the purpose of the Law. It has two chief characteristics. First, it assumes that godliness consists merely of living as closely as possible to moral laws. Legalists are right in insisting that we should keep moral laws; but they err in thinking such conformity changes our relationship with God. Many non-Christians do not lie, steal, or commit adultery. They may also abstain from movies, smoking, and drunkenness. If we define spirituality in terms of what we should *not* do, then even atheists could pass the test!

Satan doesn't mind if we equate spirituality with good works and deeds. As long as he can keep us from walking in newness of life, he doesn't care whether we take God's name in vain or not. If he can get us to believe we are righteous because we attend church on Sundays rather than watch television or surf the internet, he has won a colossal victory. He even enjoys a prayer of thanksgiving as long as it goes, "I thank God that I am not like other men who smoke, drink, and gamble, or even like this church member who drinks wine at his table." Such a person still thinks he's righteous because of what he's doing rather than because of what God has already done. To him Christ would say, "For you are like whitewashed tombs, which outwardly appear beautiful, but within are full of dead people's bones and all uncleanness. So you also outwardly appear righteous to others, but within you are full of hypocrisy and lawlessness" (Matthew 23:27–28).

Second, legalism emphasizes outward conduct almost solely to the exclusion of inward thoughts and motivations.

Since legalists do not understand the far-reaching consequences of living according to biblical exhortations, they are content to define worldliness according to a given list which specifies which amusements, entertainment, and habits are sins and to be shunned. Those who obey the list are not worldly; those who do not, are.

In one word, legalism is *self-righteousness*. It is the belief that God is satisfied with our attempt to obey a moral code. The legalist lives the Christian life (or what they think is the Christian life) by sheer willpower and is proud of their efforts.

Now we must consider in more detail the blight of legalism, especially the type that has stunted the spiritual growth of numerous Christians. Specifically, we must see the limitations and problems connected with using a code to define what Christian living really means.

## THE DANGERS OF LEGALISM

Of the three types of legalism mentioned, the second (spiritual maturity comes by the law) and the third (adding to the biblical laws) are both found in evangelical churches. Usually they exist together. Many who understand clearly that salvation comes by faith alone, believe spiritual growth is nothing more than conformity to a list of "don'ts." And in order to make certain that everyone falls into the pattern, the requirements are spelled out in more detail than the

Scriptures themselves warrant.

Sometimes those who join churches are expected to conform to certain restrictions which may limit their entertainment, habits, and lifestyles. Since such lists often vary from church to church (even within denominations) and from state to state, perceptive Christians have wondered aloud whether such sins are actually based on the Scriptures. Presumably, if these so-called taboos were condemned in Scripture, all questions regarding them would be settled once and for all. But this hasn't happened. In fact, as the years pass, the lists not only vary but become shorter.

These restrictions originally arose because of the dangers and temptations associated with some activities. As our society becomes more saturated with sensuality, the pressure to conform to the mood of our day is powerful. So two matters need emphasis. First, I am not suggesting we necessarily condone the activities which have been classified as sinful. My point is that a list of sinful activities should not be used to define worldliness. As we shall see, lists have not—and cannot—go far enough. To let a list of taboos specify worldliness is being content with too little. In fact, whenever we classify a list of activities as "worldly," we may unintentionally be lowering our standards rather than elevating them.

Second, a list of prohibitions can be of value if its limitations are properly understood. Such standards can help keep us from sin. However, we err when we tacitly assume such restrictions somehow make us righteous; we err in thinking such a list of activities can define what a Christian lifestyle really is. For this reason, we must understand the limitations of outward restrictions or else we will be guilty of reducing Christianity to a lifestyle which falls short of what God intended. Why?

Whenever we label certain questionable activities as "sin," there is the tendency to lose sight of the biblical admonitions which are to guide us in every area of conduct. For example, Christ taught that if we look at a woman to lust, we have already committed adultery in our hearts. This teaching is universally true; there are no exceptions. This one verse alone is sufficient to eliminate scores of books, movies, websites, and television shows which are designed to lead us to sensual thoughts. Parents have the responsibility to forbid their children to attend entertainment venues, social functions, or parties that foster and encourage permissiveness. All Christians should restrict themselves in those areas where they are weak and tempted to sin. When we identify one or two activities as being sinful, we often give the impression that those who do not participate in these activities are *ipso facto* living an acceptable moral life. Yet it's obvious that such a conclusion does not follow. We can be sensual without watching movies or the latest reality television show. So, while we need not condone questionable activities, we dare not give the impression that those who refrain from these activities are automatically living according to a distinctively Christian lifestyle. Of course they may be, but not necessarily.

Rules can cover only a small fraction of the situations where we might be led into sin, and of course there are no rules that can keep us from covetousness and pride. So, even though certain restrictions are commendable, they should not become a substitute for teaching the radical purity of heart which Christ demands. Abstaining from certain amusements is necessary but also very easy (we noted before that atheists could do this too); however, God's standards penetrate so much deeper, only He can give us the power to live as He intended. Christianity demands more than abstaining from a few selected sins.

Another danger in using a list of don'ts to specify worldliness is the temptation to minimize our obligation toward God. As humans, we are often satisfied to fulfill the minimum required of us—just enough to be accepted by the Christian community and pay God His dues. When we do not genuinely hunger and thirst after righteousness, we will always want to know precisely what is expected and then do only that.

The difference between outward and inward motivation can be illustrated by someone who works for an employer. If their heart is in the work, there's no looking at the clock every few minutes, unless it is to see how *much* they can do per hour. They don't mind working overtime if their schedule permits it. They delight to be at the service of their boss. But the worker who is there only for a paycheck wants to know the rules so they know how little they can do without having the wrath of their employer fall on them. At five o'clock they drop whatever they're doing and leave. If asked to help out on another project, they object with, "I wasn't hired to do this."

This attitude is exemplified by the person who asks, "How should a person tithe? Should it be ten percent of the net or gross income?" They want to know precisely what they're obligated to give. And now that God has ten percent, the other ninety percent can be spent freely. They never give more than asked. Of course, many who tithe do not do so legalistically. They joyfully give a tenth of their income to specific Christian ministries and use the other ninety percent faithfully, recognizing that it belongs to God as well. But we must be careful not to give the impression that the Christian life can be defined in terms of a given number of obligations.

A legalistic athlete dislikes football but plays the game to please the coach or to get a good raise. He wants to know precisely what the requirements are; he finds out how many practices he's permitted to skip, and he makes sure he uses his quota. Of course, it's better that he do the minimum required than nothing at all, but candidly, he finds playing football boring. His heart is somewhere else. Another athlete plays football for the love of the game. He's not concerned about the minimum requirements set down by the coach, because he goes beyond what's expected. He doesn't try to see how little he can get by with and still be accepted by his teammates. His heart is in the game. Both athletes keep the rules of their club, but one is legalistic and another is not. Question: How are you playing the Christian life?

A third danger in making a list of sinful activities is that contradictions and petty distinctions are almost inevitable. Back in the 70s, the late author Joe Bayly suggested that God must have a sense of humor; surely He must have laughed when Christians bought television sets to get caught up on the movies they had missed during the past twenty years.

Some Christians never play sports on Sunday or attend games but will watch the football game at home on Sunday afternoon. Smoking is condemned because our body is the temple of the Holy Spirit, but one who lives on insufficient sleep is considered diligent. Gluttony, which harms the body extensively, is only mentioned in jest. Such inconsistencies could be multiplied indefinitely.

Faced with these difficulties, some Christians have mistakenly concluded that all rules should be dropped in order to be consistent. But this attitude displays a misunderstanding of the issues involved. The solution is not to approve of all activities listed simply to be consistent. Rather, the inconsistencies only remind us that it's impossible to specify on a consistent basis how a given scriptural principle is to be applied to a given situation. The taboos are not necessarily wrong but merely inadequate. So rather than multiplying the number of rules or increasing the list of don'ts, we must return to the fundamental principles and show how they are to be applied in all situations. This may necessitate abstaining from certain habits, but it will also include much more. Each Christian must go beyond the restrictions of their church to determine what God expects of them personally. In some cases, there may be personal differences, but a Christian lifestyle must be rooted in the guidelines and principles revealed in the Scriptures. As will be shown, principles can be consistently applied.

What it boils down to is this: Can we solve the problems of legalism by changing our standards or by changing people? Perhaps if we begin to see the thrust of God's commands, we will understand why the Christian life is more than conformity to a given behavior pattern; it's more than a life lived by sheer willpower. It's a radical transformation calculated to change us from the inside out. Briefly, it is God doing what the best laws and rules cannot do; it is God giving us Christ's righteousness as well as qualities of character that transcend human ability. A return to the basics of Scripture will be a return to the living God.

## LIVING UNDER GRACE

Since no rules—including the moral law—can produce spirituality, some Christians conclude that it's unnecessary to be subject to any restrictions. This attitude is often found among those who have been delivered from excessive legalism. They finally realize that spirituality does not come by the Law, so they have a "liberated syndrome" which makes them disdain all restrictions. Perhaps they have seen many who believed they were righteous because they abstained from the list of sins on the church consecration pledge. So when they (the supposedly liberated Christians) finally see that spirituality is produced by submission to the Holy Spirit, they misuse their new freedom. They reason thus: If spirituality is not generated by abstaining from certain amusements, entertainment, social activities, or sensual pleasures, why should I refrain from these activities? On the surface, anything seems permissible. This is why Paul warned, "For you were called to freedom, brothers. Only do not use your freedom as an opportunity for the flesh, but through love serve one another" (Galatians 5:13).

It is true that the entire Mosaic law, including the Ten Commandments, was done away in Christ (2 Corinthians 3:7–11). But this doesn't mean we can do as we please. In this age, we are under the law of Christ which differs from the Mosaic law in at least three ways. First, we are under more stringent demands. It's relatively easy to keep the commandment "You shall not murder" (Exodus 20:13), but Christ taught that hating your brother means you are a murderer at heart (Matthew 5:22). We cannot solve the problem of legalism by abolishing laws! The first step in turning from legalism is to realize that the attitude of our heart must correspond with outward conduct. The Mosaic law emphasized overt sin; those who kept it outwardly erroneously believed they had met God's requirements.

Christ's definition of sin penetrates far deeper than a list of sins on a membership card. It goes to our inner desires, motivations, and secret thoughts. His teaching condemns us so completely that we can never again think we have any righteousness of our own.

There are literally hundreds of commands in the New Testament that are humanly impossible to keep. We are called to live in a manner radically distinct from the accepted conduct of mediocre Christianity. Facing the impossible, we are driven to Christ for forgiveness and superhuman ability. God has not relaxed His standards, and neither can we.

Second, the motivation under the Mosaic law was, "Obey and you will be blessed." Today we have a different incentive. God has already freely blessed us with all spiritual blessings (Ephesians 1:3). Now we are to serve Him out of sheer gratitude for what Christ has *already* done for us. True Christianity can never be reduced to a pattern of behavior agreed upon by a committee.

Have you ever wondered why one characteristic of legalism is a critical attitude? The simple reason is that legalists are never motivated by joy. A legalist will do only what is expected, and when they do go beyond the call of duty, it's to exalt themselves. Their heart is not in what they do. As a result, they envy those who are getting by and not toeing the line. They resent others who enjoy activities they secretly would like to do. They like specific rules so they know what they're obligated to do; then they have the satisfaction of knowing they have scrupulously done their duty.

This is why there will be some surprises at the judgment seat. Christ told a parable about some laborers who had agreed to work in a vineyard for a denarius a day. But those who had been hired at the third hour received the same amount as those who were hired at the eleventh. The first group, who had worked all day, complained because they received no more than those who had come later. Yet the landowner answered, "Am I not allowed to do what I choose with what belongs to me? Or do you begrudge my generosity? So the last will be first, and the first last" (Matthew 20:15–16). Some self-righteous individuals think God is pleased with them because they have spent more time in His vineyard. They forget that God owes us nothing. Any rewards we receive are of His grace, and even after we have given our best, we are still unprofitable servants and have done only our duty.

The motivation for legalists is the Law; they plod along hoping that someday their efforts will pay off. They take pride in their faithfulness in "serving the Lord," even though their neighbors have seen no reasons as to why they should want to serve that same Lord.

Third, living under grace means God's supernatural power is readily available. In the Old Testament, believers did not have the Holy Spirit indwelling them (though some were given the Spirit temporarily to complete certain God-given tasks). Since the day of Pentecost, every believer is permanently indwelt by the Holy Spirit. Because of this, believers are able to have character traits that God alone can produce in us. We can obey restrictions by willpower, but we cannot live the Christian life by willpower alone. A Christian lifestyle is the character of Christ reproduced in us. It is living supernaturally in a world convinced that the supernatural is a relic of past imaginations.

When Paul listed the nine fruits of the Spirit in Galatians, he added, "against such things there is no law" (5:23). There can be no law prohibiting such qualities; and I might add, there is no law which can produce them either!

True, restrictions can neither produce nor guarantee spirituality, but if we submit to the Spirit, we will discover enablement to meet the demands of the Law more fully than before. As Paul put it, God sent His Son "in order that the righteous requirement of the law might be fulfilled in us, who walk not according to the flesh but according to the Spirit" (Romans 8:4). When we are controlled by the Spirit, we will fulfill the Law but in a different way and for a different reason than the legalist who believes his human effort is all that God requires.

To summarize, the good is sometimes the enemy of the best. Legalists misuse something good (the Law or valid restrictions), and this prevents them from seeing the new life Christ came to bring. The answer to legalism is not to abolish restrictions. Rather, it is to recognize Christ gives us the only righteousness available and that the possibility of living the Christian life is dependent on His power. Drudgery must be exchanged for delight, self-righteousness for humility, and criticism for commitment.

Anything less than this reduces Christianity to a life that a worldly Christian can live.

## LIVING BY PRINCIPLES

If the Bible writers listed which activities were sins and which were not, the Bible would soon be out of date. As new amusements, entertainment, and pleasures were invented, any list compiled in the first century would soon become obsolete.

But the Bible is timeless; its teachings can be applied in every age in all cultures. Its commands are directed primarily to our hearts, and in this way, it escapes the limitations of an arbitrary list of sins. Our behavior should be based on its teachings, commands, exhortations, and doctrine. Such an approach will give us a solid foundation for our conduct in a day of relativism and worldly pressures.

In a way, it's a good thing certain practices (watching football games on Sunday) and certain amusements (playing pool) are no longer taboo. Many Christians are finally realizing that Christianity is more than a list of don'ts. However, along with this realization, a new danger has been created. By rejecting the taboos of the past, many Christians are also rejecting the basic principles which originally gave rise to those taboos. To use a cliche, the baby is thrown out with the bath water. If an activity is now permissible, there are those who think they have the right to do it without any questions asked.

If their church approves movies, they attend the theater or binge watch television without exercising discretion. They never stop to evaluate their actions or even pause to ask whether the amusements and entertainment they enjoy are positively helping them to fulfill the will of God in their lives. As the taboos are abandoned, they have no moral or spiritual basis for their conduct. All they know is that what was once wrong is now right, and what is wrong today may be right tomorrow. As the Christian community sinks, they sink along with it.

For example, when television was first invented, many

Christians were opposed to it. Later, television received acceptance. But along with that acceptance, the principles which led to its original rejections were abandoned. In other words, when television was approved among Christians, it was accepted *in toto*, without specific biblical principles governing its use. Today, with the plethora of cable channels and internet-based programs, children are permitted to watch practically all types of shows; parents waste time watching worthless programs, and hours are squandered that should be spent with the family. Because the evangelical community was not trained to apply biblical principles to situations (such decisions were made by those who formulated the rules), entertainment delivered through a television or the internet has turned out to be a god for many. Little can be said to such people without them responding, "What's wrong with television (or the internet)?" And, of course, the answer is "nothing." But some Christians have forgotten that such technology, used without a consistent application of biblical principles, can lead to spiritual disaster.

In South America, upon leaving an old Catholic church every Sunday morning, the congregation turned to face an old wall, genuflected, made the sign of the cross, then left. A visitor was curious to find out why they did this, especially because the wall was bare. When he asked the people why they did it, they answered that their parents and grandparents had done this, so they did it too. Years later, when the church was torn down, the workmen discovered beneath the many layers of paint on that wall, a beautiful painting of the Virgin Mary. The original congregation had bowed to the beautiful painting, but the succeeding generations had simply perpetuated the tradition, even though the reason for their religious rite had long since vanished beneath the dust and paint.

Some Christians copy the conduct of their friends or church. When the Christian community changes its standards, they do too, but they never know why. They are content to blindly follow the questionable guidance of others. The penetrating teachings of the New Testament have either been jettisoned or buried beneath debris.

Many Christians object to a given list of sins, not because they want to elevate Christian conduct to the radical level of the New Testament, but because they would like to lower their personal standards. Maybe they suspect that they're missing out on some pleasures, perhaps even sensual ones. So they criticize the taboos of the past for the wrong reasons. Their convictions continually shift on the quicksand of moral indifference.

Our only hope is obedience to the teachings of the New Testament; our fate depends on whether we are willing to become one of Christ's disciples in the fullest sense. Then we will search our hearts, motives, and affections. Anything that mars our fellowship with God will be recognized as sin. We will discipline and restrict ourselves in matters that can never be included in an official statement on worldliness. Like Christ, we will not seek to please ourselves but will want to please God alone.

What else would happen if we began to live according to the teachings of the New Testament? What would the implications be if we actually did set our affections on things above and not on things of the earth? What if we actually did seek first the kingdom of God and His righteousness? Or what if we did yield our bodies as sacrifices to the living God? And if we prayed without ceasing?

The consequences of such obedience are devastating to someone who does nothing more than live up to a list of rules. Let me suggest three effects this perspective would have on our conduct. First, we would evaluate *everything* we do in the light of God's demands; we would be sensitive to His control in every area of our lives. Even wholesome activities would have to be abandoned when they overshadow the weightier matters of discipleship.

For example, even sports such as football, basketball, and tennis are sin when they become the consuming passion of our lives. There are those who justify their interest in such games because they derive their standards from the church, which, of course, approves of such recreation. But what we must realize is that even such neutral activities are sin when they occupy time, attention, and energy that should be directed toward God, our families, and our friends. It seems odd that some who have difficulty remembering even the most familiar passage of Scripture find they are able to recite the batting averages of several baseball players. We remember those things we are interested in. And where our treasure is, there our heart will be also (Matthew 6:21).

Second, we would also learn that we cannot specify what activities are legitimate for others when the issues are not entirely clear. My weakness may not be yours; yours might not be mine. Something which leads me astray might not have a similar effect on you. We would each have to determine before God and the Scriptures what He wants *us* to do. We wouldn't be critical of others who don't fit into our prescribed pattern. When we did see faults in others, we would help them in love rather than with self-righteous condemnation.

Finally, something else equally important would happen: We would begin to see the utter impossibility of living the Christian life. God's desire for inward purity would loom so great that we would be driven to Him for supernatural ability. We would see that He demands so much that only He can supply what He demands!

The standards we had formerly followed would shrivel in comparison to His stringent demands. Petty distinctions would pale in comparison to the weightier matters of honesty, purity, and the fruit of the Spirit. We would feel helpless, morally weak, and wholly inadequate. And this would be the beginning of a totally different perspective of Christianity; a perspective that would once again make God a necessity for living a Christian life.

This perspective will help us realize that those who live in the power of the Holy Spirit have not been given the short end of the stick. Christ has not trapped us into being good while others can have a good time. His restrictions were given to show us more keenly our need of Him. Once we have seen the dimension of the Christian life, we would no longer believe Satan's lie, namely, that Christ came to take the fun out of life.

We would understand that a Christian is more than a sinner minus his sins; never again would we settle for living according to a pattern of behavior by sheer willpower. There would be a supernatural aspect to our lives defying human explanation. And perhaps for the first time, we would understand what Christ meant when He said that He came to give us *life* and to give it more abundantly.

Then if we were arrested for being a Christian, there would finally be enough evidence to convict us. Our lifestyle would demonstrate that we are living in dependence on the living God. *That* is the first prerequisite for genuine Christian conduct!

## QUESTIONS FOR DISCUSSION

1. How are positive and negative commands in the Word of God helpful to us?

2. Define legalism.

3. Name three forms of legalism found in the Scriptures. Describe the characteristics of each.

4. What are the two chief misunderstandings about legalism?

5. Discuss the dangers of legalism.

6. Read Galatians 5:13. To what extent may we exercise our Christian liberty?

7. In what three ways does the law of Christ differ from the Mosaic laws? Discuss each difference.

8. Why is it important that our behavior be based on biblical teachings? What three effects will living by biblical principles have on our conduct?

CHAPTER EIGHT

# HOW DOLLARS
# CAN MAKE SENSE

Money does talk. Listen carefully to what it says:

    Dug from the mountain side

    Or washed in the glen,

    Servant am I or master of men.

    Earn me, I bless you;

    Steal me, I curse you;

    Grasp me and hold me,

    A fiend shall possess you.

    Lie for me, die for me,

    Covet me, take me—

    Angel or devil,

    I'm just what you make me.

                             —Author unknown

Everything God has given us is a test of our loyalty. But our attitude toward money is an especially accurate barometer of our relationship to the world. In fact, no man who loves money can simultaneously love God. John wrote, "But if anyone has the world's goods and sees his brother in need, yet closes his heart against him, how does God's love abide in him?" (1 John 3:17). To love money is to hate God.

Often the subject of money is misunderstood or ignored. Sometimes, believers become weary of hearing about stewardship, or they misunderstand what the Scriptures teach concerning their paycheck. As a result, their spiritual development is stifled.

## GOD'S VIEW OF YOUR MONEY

One of the most common misconceptions about stewardship (using our money for God) buried deeply in our minds is that it is a good idea—for the rich. Consequently, we excuse ourselves. If we had a million dollars we are convinced we'd give God half of it. But the truth is, we wouldn't—unless we are already giving a generous proportion of our income *now*. Perhaps only a mental explosion can pry us loose from the notion that we should not bother trying to understand the scriptural principles of giving and buying because we don't have much to spend or give. Such reasoning has two deceptions. First, it assumes God considers giving from a utilitarian viewpoint (how much actual good our money does), rather than from a spiritual standpoint (the attitude in which it was given). From the standpoint of *results*, the widow in Mark 12: 41–44, who gave two small copper coins, accomplished nothing. How much gold did her two coins buy to complete the temple decorations? How many priests were able to buy a meal with what she put in? None. But Jesus said she gave more than those who put in enough money to *do* something, such as to finish the temple, to pay the priests, and hopefully to help the poor.

A hundred dollars will buy a missionary some equipment. Fifty will help pay the utility bills of the church. A couple of dollars buys a few stamps. Two pennies? *Spare the effort of putting them into the offering plate. Give when you can make it worthwhile so that something can be done with the amount.* Does such reasoning sound familiar? This philosophy lurks in the back of many minds, like the Pharisees who thought God wanted money—lots of it—so that something worthwhile could be accomplished on Earth. But Jesus said the two small copper coins were worth more in God's book than a generous amount. With that philosophy of arithmetic, a certified accountant would lose his job in a day.

But God doesn't count money by adding it together or by calculating how much it will buy. Those who give much without sacrifice are reckoned as having given little; those who give from all their living are reckoned as having given much. Without that basic understanding, we've missed the purpose of giving—and we've missed it by a mile.

The second deception in this philosophy is that we are poor while others are rich. Certainly some do have larger bank accounts than us, and these people look to others who have even more than they do, and so it goes *ad nauseum*. But we forget that millions upon millions have less than any of you reading this. In many countries of the world, it would take a day to earn enough money to buy this book. In some places of the world, naked children eat crumbs of bread and decayed meat found in alleys. For them, anyone who can afford a pair of shoes is wealthy. We have become so tainted by the affluence of our day that we have lost sight of what God has given us. Many of us have never had to pray, "Give us our daily bread." We spend more time counting our calories than we do our blessings.

One of the most accurate barometers of our spiritual maturity is the way we use our money. In the Scriptures, a wrong attitude toward money is directly associated with worldliness and godlessness. Think of the money in your pocket right now. Two dollars? Two cents? How you spend it may reflect whether you are in the world though not of it. If we use it properly, we will not lose it; if we misuse it, it will be snatched from us. Like the rich fool, we will have gained the whole world (or tried to) but will have lost our own soul.

The most basic truth that God wants to teach us

regarding our money is that *all* of it belongs to Him. Whenever we use it selfishly, we rob God, since it rightfully belongs to Him. The first step in becoming detached from the love of money is to recognize that everything we have is His, and therefore, we must consciously return our bank accounts to God. This will rid us of the notion that we can give God His portion on Sunday, and having fulfilled our duty, spend the rest on ourselves. Many of us Christians still have two separate compartments in our minds. God gets His share, perhaps ten percent or less, and we get the rest. God gets one part, and we get nine. God can use His part as He wishes, and we can use our part as we wish. What more can God ask, especially with rising inflation? Answer: He asks for it all.

Obviously we should give a part of our money to the church, missionaries, and other worthy causes. But let us remember that God will not merely judge us on the basis of what we gave but also on the basis of what we did with what we kept for ourselves. That too belongs to Him. We will be accountable for every dollar we have earned.

How then should we handle God's money? For one thing, it means learning to depend on God for wisdom to use it in the best possible way. Certainly God may want us to have a new vacuum cleaner, car, or winter coat, but since we are buying these items with God's money, they in turn also belong to Him. What we spend on ourselves is just as much God's as what we put into the offering plate.

Look at it this way. If your employer gave you $100 and asked you to spend it wisely and give an account to him for it, you would spend it very carefully. At the end of the day, you would give him an itemized list of what you had bought, and you would be prepared to justify every expenditure. But if the $100 was yours, you could squander it or even lose it without having to answer for your actions.

When we realize our money is lent to us by God, we will be careful how we spend it. As we see others who are in need, we will learn to distinguish between our own needs (the basic necessities) and our wants. God may permit us to have some luxuries and to spend His money for our enjoyment, but we won't insist on such privileges. Having food and clothing, we will be content.

The advertising industry has created the impression that luxuries are necessities and wants are actually needs. We can enjoy whatever we like now and pay later. This desire for things has become so powerful that even Christians have become the victims of endless monthly payments and high interest rates. Credit cards make it almost impossible to bypass a bargain. Eventually, we are drowned in a swamp of debts. What's the answer?

Part of the solution is to recognize our money belongs to God and therefore, we have no right to covet the conveniences and luxuries others might have. To borrow money for a wise investment may be necessary; but to go into debt for a luxury is foolishness. God may deprive us of certain wants—as well as necessities—in order to teach us to trust Him. Too often our credit card becomes a substitute for our heavenly Father who knows in advance what we need. The first principle of finances is to consciously give all you have to God and depend on Him for wisdom on how to spend what He has lent you, whether little or much.

Christ taught another financial principle by means of a parable. An unjust steward used the possessions of his master to make friends so that when he was fired, he could depend on these friends to accept him into their home (Luke 16:1–13). Christ taught we should use money to make friendships that have lasting value, but even more important, He added, "One who is faithful in a very little is also faithful in much, and one who is dishonest in a very little is also dishonest in much" (16:10). Money is the real test of a person's character. This is why God is not so concerned whether we have little or whether we have much; He tells us our attitude will be the basis of His evaluation. If we are faithful with two dollars, we will be faithful with two hundred. If we are unfaithful with one dollar, God knows we will be unfaithful with two.

In another parable, Christ taught the same principle even more forcibly. A worthless slave had all of his money taken away from him because he didn't use his master's money wisely (Luke 19:12–26). The servants who invested their master's money profitably were given authority over a proportionate number of cities. But the servant who hid his master's money without investing it had his money snatched from him and given to another. Christ's point is clear: In God's kingdom, we will be given responsibility only to the extent that we were faithful with God's money on Earth. Treasures in heaven are accumulated by our attitude to our treasures (or lack of them) on Earth.

Sometimes we associate heavenly rewards with winning people to Christ, teaching Sunday school, or memorizing Scripture. And if we have done these things in dependence upon Christ, we shall not lose our reward. But how many of us believe our heavenly riches will be directly related to the way in which we invested our nickels, dimes, and dollars on Earth? This jingle by an unknown poet puts it accurately:

> It's not what you'd do with a million
> If riches should be your lot
> It's what you are doing at present
> With the dollar and quarter you've got.

We're tempted to ask: But why does God choose money as the test of our loyalty to Him? Why not faithfulness in church attendance or using our other "talents"? Certainly these related gifts enter into the total picture of God's evaluation of us. But money is emphasized in Scripture simply because our temptation to love it is inexplicably powerful. The fact is that few people have the spiritual resources needed to be both wealthy and godly. As Christ vividly explained, " It is easier for a camel to go through the eye of a needle than for a rich person to enter the kingdom of God" (Mark 10:25).

Paul wrote, "But those who desire to be rich fall into temptation, into a snare, into many senseless and harmful desires that plunge people into ruin and destruction" (1 Timothy 6:9). A Christian man who works at a prominent bank in downtown Chicago and is responsible for counting millions of dollars, has said employees were constantly being fired for theft, even though they knew they were being checked for honesty. The temptation was too great, even though being caught was inevitable.

Money is only one part of a person's life, but the love of it is the root of all sorts of evil (1 Timothy 6:10). Many Christians are unaware of how deceitful wealth (or the lack of it) can be. Under the guise of having to earn a living, all sorts of selfishness is tolerated. The rich are vulnerable to sin because they are tempted to get more; those who have little are determined to cling selfishly to what they already have. The legitimate need to earn a living turns out to be the central motivation in some lives where God is consulted only in the case of emergencies.

Most warnings in Scripture are directed to all people,

rich or poor. The basic problem is not wealth or lack of it, but rather the human heart. The rich may face unique problems because of their desire to get more; but the poor face the same temptations in their desire to get rich. So in God's eyes, the rich as well as the poor are tested by their attitude toward what they have as well as toward what they would like to have. Money talks. It speaks either the language of the world or the language of God.

Let's suppose we knew in advance a certain company would go bankrupt within a short time. We would never invest our money in such a risky venture. We would choose a reliable bank with guaranteed interest. Yet, whenever we use our money as though it's our own, whenever we spend it for the things we want without any consideration of its rightful Owner, we have invested it in the system of this world, a stock market that has already collapsed. Our bankruptcy is as inevitable as the sunrise.

In Christ's day, there were three primary sources of wealth: clothes, grain, and gold. Christ predicted that moths would eat the clothes, rust (blight and rot) would eat the grain, and thieves would steal the gold. Even though our wealth today might be more secure, the Scriptures teach that we have brought nothing into this world and it is equally certain that we will carry nothing out. To invest our money in the world is to have lived in vain. One day when Alexander the Great was looking dejected, one of his generals said to him, "You have conquered the world; what more can you ask?" To which Alexander replied, "You are right, but what I have will not last!"

The alternative is to invest our money in the bank of heaven which is not affected by the variable trends of the Dow Jones Industrial Average. We can spend our money in such a way that the dividends won't even be affected by inflation. God has ordained that we should give money toward the needs of others to display our love and to weld us together more closely in the work He has given us here on Earth. Let us consider more specifically what this involves.

## GIVING

Preacher to Farmer: If you had two farms, would you give one of them to God?

Farmer: Of course, you know I would!

Preacher: If you had two thousand dollars, would you give one thousand to God?

Farmer: Why certainly I would!

Preacher: If you had two pigs—

Farmer: Now preacher, that's not fair; you know I have two pigs.

The subject of giving often makes Christians a bit uneasy, or else it puts them to sleep. We have been so bombarded with letters, offerings, and solicitations that we can't sort them out. Since most of us find it easier to spend money than to give it, we prefer to be immune to the constant pleas for needed funds here and help with deficits there. Someone has suggested that it's time for a moratorium on giving.

Maybe it is. At least we should pause long enough to find out what the Bible teaches on the subject. And in the process, we might be awakened to realize that God has some pointed suggestions about how we should use what He has given us.

Today there are a host of worthy churches and organizations in need of funds. In desperation, some of them have hired teams of experts to analyze their constituency and evaluate the financial assets of a given community. The experts' job description is clear: extract the needed funds from the constituency, using any method proven to work. Then promote the program as "honoring to God," since this money will be used to prop up His interests in the world.

One man, hired to raise a few million dollars for one Christian organization, passed this tip to local pastors. "We've found that people give more when they fill out their pledges in the presence of someone else." Undoubtedly, they do. At least Ananias and Sapphira did.

While I've been writing this, two brochures have come to my desk with information on how to raise money for churches, schools, and civic organizations. The methods have been proven and are guaranteed to succeed. One brochure boasts that with proper techniques, almost any church can practically double its church budget. Trained fundraising consultants can calculate in advance which methods will achieve the desired results.

We shouldn't dispute their claims. It is true that churches can increase their budget, mission boards can operate in the black, and Christian schools can pay their faculty members by using hard sell and direct appeals. Nor do we suggest that such organizations are unworthy of proper financial support. Hundreds of evangelical churches and organizations are dedicated to proclaim the gospel. Many of these are dependent upon the gifts of the Christian community. But should we succumb to the financial burdens and use modern techniques to ask Christians to share their wealth? Or might it be that a lack of funds is a discipleship issue? In short, what does the Bible have to say about giving?

Since most Christians immediately think of tithing when money or stewardship is mentioned, perhaps the first question we should ask is whether tithing is a requirement for the New Testament church. The answer is no. The word *tithe* is found eight times in the New Testament. In the Gospels, it's used with reference to the Pharisees who were tithing only to fulfill their obligations to the Mosaic law (Matthew 23:23; Luke 11:42; 18:12). The only other occurrences of the word are in Hebrews 7 where the priesthood of Melchizedek is shown to be superior to that of Levi. If tithing were a requirement, we would expect such a commandment to be found in the New Testament. Several chapters are devoted to the subject of giving in the New Testament; yet tithing is not mentioned.

The tithe was a part of the Mosaic law, which was never given to Gentiles and which has been done away in Christ (2 Corinthians 3:7–13). Even the oft quoted words of Malachi 3 are expressly addressed to the sons of Jacob. To the Jews, God promised material prosperity if they would bring tithes and offerings and make proper use of their land. But today, prosperity is not necessarily a sign of godly living, and godly living doesn't guarantee prosperity. Those who have not seen the basic difference between God's dealings with the nation Israel and His relationship to the church have falsely concluded that God is obligated to bless us materially if we give a certain percentage of our income to Him. There have been numerous books which suggest we can, if we wish, become wealthy by giving. This was true for the nation Israel, living in the land God had provided, but no such promises are made in the New Testament for the church in this age.

Furthermore, in the Old Testament, tithing was a form of taxation imposed on all the Israelites. In fact, there were at least three tithes. One was for the maintenance of the

Levites, since they were responsible for the work of the tabernacle (Leviticus 27:30–33). There was also the tithe for the national feasts and sacrifices (Deuteronomy 12:5–6; 14:22–24), and finally there was a tithe every third year used for the poor of the land (Deuteronomy 14:28–29). This means an Israelite might be expected to give more than twenty percent of his income to support the various observances God commanded. This was mandatory. Over and above this, he was still to bring gifts as a freewill offering to God (Malachi 3:8–10). As far as *giving* is concerned, there is no amount specified by God, either in the Old Testament or the New.

Many Christian leaders admit privately that tithing is not a New Testament requirement but justify an emphasis on tithing by saying God demanded ten percent under the Law, therefore, it's not asking too much to require at least that much if not more under grace. Such reasoning is based on fear: If tithing isn't taught as a requirement, then Christians might end up giving nothing at all. So to ensure the fact that some money will flow into the depleted coffers, tithing is taught despite its lack of scriptural support.

Such reasoning has two flaws. First, when people give for a wrong motive, such offerings are unacceptable to God. This can be shown by the frequent references in the Old Testament to God's loathing the offerings of His people (Isaiah 1:12–15). The second error is failing to see that when believers give with proper motivation, they will gladly give beyond ten percent. Therefore, in the long run, an emphasis on tithing hinders rather than increases the amount of money given.

Detailed instructions on giving are found in 2 Corinthians 8 and 9. Paul begins his discussion by using the Christians of Macedonia as an example of giving that is acceptable to God. The Macedonians were devastated by an earthquake and had gone through a series of tragedies. Yet they gave extensively out of their poverty to the needy saints at Jerusalem (2 Corinthians 8:1–6). Paul says they didn't merely give according to their ability but gave even *beyond* their ability. No one had demanded anything of them. There was no requirement they were expected to meet. In fact, they *begged* for the opportunity to participate in the support of other saints (vv. 3–4). In our day, such an attitude is so rare that if we found a church pleading for the privilege of giving to the needs of others, we would consider the members odd if not fanatical. What could be the secret of their generosity?

Paul writes, "They gave themselves first to the Lord" (v. 5). Perhaps the reason they were a model church in giving is because they were a model church in dedication. If Paul had taught tithing as a requirement, he would have dampened their motivation. Or at least such teaching would have obscured the true purpose of why they wanted to give. But there was no reason to require anything of them. They gave without any compulsion and gave beyond what was humanly expected.

The Macedonians' enthusiasm for helping the needy was not shared by the Corinthians. An offering had been started among them, but it hadn't been completed. Titus was being sent back to them, and Paul wanted to encourage the Corinthians to give with the right motivation. He stated clearly that he wasn't demanding that they give (v. 8), for this would be inconsistent with the kind of motivation God accepts. Paul wanted them to be motivated by the example of Christ, who, "though he was rich, yet for your sake he became poor, so that you by his poverty might become rich" (v. 9).

The most fundamental principle of giving is that we should give because Christ gave. We shouldn't give because we were asked to, nor because we have to stick to our budget. We should give because we want to express our love for Christ by our gifts. Christ is our example.

Let's take a closer look at a few of the principles of giving. Paul writes, "Each one must give as he has decided in his heart, not reluctantly or under compulsion, for God loves a cheerful giver" (2 Corinthians 9:7). First, we are not to give with a stingy attitude. Money given with resentment doesn't honor God. It might help meet the budget, but this doesn't justify the gift. Since God has given to us so generously, it's an insult to give to Him grudgingly. Consequently, it's better to not give at all than to regret having to part with such hard-earned cash. Some Christians think of giving as one of those painful experiences we must endure if we want to receive the benefits of the church. With such an attitude, it's better to look straight ahead and let the offering plate pass by.

Just to emphasize how important our attitude is, Paul says that if our hearts are right, we are acceptable to God even when we cannot give anything, "If you are really eager to give, then it isn't important how much you have to give. God wants you to give what you have, not what you haven't" (2 Corinthians 8:12, TLB). As mentioned earlier, God is more concerned with our heart attitude than He is with the amount we give. That is why the widow who gave two small copper coins gave more than those who paid for the gold furnishings in the temple.

Second, Paul says we should not give out of compulsion. We should not give because we feel forced to give. Giving should not be something imposed upon us by a fundraising committee that reaches its objectives by having someone else present when we fill out our pledges. Though such "gimmicks" may work, it is the heart of the giver which is important. They must give because they truly—and joyfully—want to give to God's work.

It follows that giving should therefore be a private

matter between each individual and God. In 1 Corinthians 16:2, Paul emphasized each person should put aside and save some money for the church. In the Greek, a reflexive pronoun translated literally "to himself" indicates the gift was to be kept in a private deposit. Out of this, the believer should distribute to specific causes, as well as give to the ministry of the church on the first day of the week.

Whenever one's giving becomes public knowledge, there is the temptation to judge others, to make unfavorable comparisons (as well as favorable ones), and we are forced to give out of compulsion. Like the Pharisees who gave to be noticed, there is the danger that the privilege of giving will degenerate into a carnal duty.

A third principle is giving proportionately. In 1 Corinthians 16:2, Paul writes that we should give as God has prospered us. Understandably, those who have much will be able to give a greater amount than those who have little. There is nothing wrong with deciding on a certain percentage of our income which should be given to the Lord's work in the church or other evangelical causes.

Since no percentage is stipulated, it could be ten, fifteen, or fifty percent—or even more. To choose ten percent is not wrong, just as long as it's not done dutifully as a required "tithe." In other words, many who do tithe do not do so legalistically; they don't give out of necessity or do they give grudgingly. But we err when we choose a certain percentage and maintain that same fraction year after year without any further consideration.

Paul seems to imply that on the Lord's Day, we ought to decide how much to lay aside for that week. Many believers simply give a certain amount on Sunday and never stop to evaluate what they should do in a specific situation. They have fallen into such a rut they never even think about consulting the Lord to find out what He might want them to give. This doesn't mean we should give spasmodically or just according to any impulse we might have. It does mean we should be sensitive to the proportion we give, being ready to increase it as the Lord enables us to. Churches often discover their income from the offerings remains the same year after year, even though the members' standard of living has been rising. While increases come in salary, there are often no increases in giving. The solution is not to hire a team of experts to collect the needed funds; rather we must see stinginess as carnality displayed in a concrete form. Unless we move insensitive believers to spiritual maturity, we have not done anything worthy of eternal reward, even if we reach our budget by using clever fundraising programs.

Then what should churches do when the needed money is not available? What should missionary societies do when they don't have enough to send to missionaries? Do these needs justify some coercion? A dollar given grudgingly might mean the giver will lose his reward, but it will help get the gospel to the ends of the earth. At least that's the way we are tempted to reason.

Let's remember that it is legitimate to make needs known. Some godly men of the past never shared the needs of their work with others but shared them with God alone. God honored their faith, and often their needs were met miraculously. However, the apostle Paul spoke openly about the needs of the saints at Jerusalem. In order to give intelligently, it is necessary to know what is needed, where the gift is going, and what it is intended to accomplish. Needs can be made known—there is nothing wrong with that. And we might add that the laborer is worthy of his hire. It's a shame for a spiritual leader to live in poverty while his constituency lives in wealth.

Beyond this, Scripture does not allow us to argue further. We can't demand a certain sum because of a deficit. After the needs have been exposed, we have to face a question: Is this work (church, mission board, outreach, etc.) of God? If it is our own work, we had better get money from somewhere; if the work is God's, it is *His* responsibility to put it upon the hearts of His children to help meet the need.

These last few paragraphs don't mean we should be unconcerned if churches and worthy Christian organizations collapse for lack of funds. When this happens, it's a sad commentary on our day. Even wealthy Christians are often miserly in their support of the church. But my plea is, rather than letting the shortage of funds drive us to promotional gimmicks that would go beyond scriptural principles, let the shortage of funds drive us to our knees for our churches, missionary programs, and country. God is trying to tell us something through the many existing needs, but let us not respond in the wrong way. Let us repent of our carnality, seek His face, and depend on Him alone. He will honor such faith.

## QUESTIONS FOR DISCUSSION

1. What is one of the most common misconceptions about stewardship? What two deceptions do we find imbedded in that misconception?

2. What basic truth does God want to teach us about money? How will that truth help us to better handle our money?

3. Read Luke 16:1–13 and 19:12–26. What financial principle did Jesus teach us with these two parables?

CHAPTER NINE

# MODERN FIG LEAVES

Do you dress like a Christian? Perhaps the question should be even more basic: Should Christians dress differently than society? Do clothes have anything to do with worldliness?

Ever since Adam and Eve sewed fig leaves together, clothing has been a part of our heritage. Presumably, if they had not sinned, clothing would not have become a necessity. But after Adam and Eve sinned, they tried to hide their guilt by cowering in the bushes; they also tried to cover their shame with fig leaves.

Now that sin was in the world, God approved of Adam and Eve's desire for clothing. The Almighty exchanged their fig leaves for clothes made of skins. From then on, clothes were needed not only to cover the shame of bodies affected by sin but also as an aid to preserving moral purity. Modesty had then become necessary in our fallen world.

Of course, wearing clothes doesn't ensure modesty.

Clothing worn to appeal to the imagination may be more seductive in our country than the accepted semi-nudity of some remote cultures.

This, however, doesn't mean we should be indifferent to current pressures toward making public nudity acceptable. In American culture, such trends are directly related to sexual permissiveness and sensuality. Some mistakenly assume that rejecting the inhibitions of the past is the path to true freedom, but the effects of sin cannot be easily ignored. Shedding clothes can neither obliterate guilt nor can it erase shame. Those who seek freedom by permissiveness are led further into moral bondage.

A discussion of clothing is not merely a discussion of cultural acceptance. For the Christian, it is also a discussion of what the Bible teaches about clothing and our attitude toward it.

In the Old Testament, God gave a command, "A woman shall not wear a man's garment, nor shall a man put on a woman's cloak, for whoever does these things is an abomination to the LORD your God" (Deuteronomy 22:5). This doesn't mean a woman should never wear slacks. This command was directed to the Israelites, along with hundreds of other detailed laws, for the purpose of preserving the peculiarity of the sexes. Every invasion of the natural distinctions between men and women violates God's order. This command prohibits transvestism (the adoption of the dress and behavior of the opposite sex), something that is taking our culture by storm today.

Gender-neutral clothing stores are becoming popular. Popular hairstyles blur the natural distinctions between the sexes (1 Corinthians 11:14–15). Since clothing itself is morally neutral and since hairstyles are directly related to cultural acceptance, it would be easy to conclude that gender-neutral trends have no great moral significance. But they do. Disregarding the distinctions between men and women is symptomatic of moral deviation. Although both sexes are equal, they have distinct functions and roles.

Clothes and hairstyles can communicate identity. Back in the 1960s, when the hippie movement began, the unofficial sign of membership for males was shoulder-length hair. Then, as longer hairstyles were more widely accepted among men, the length of hair no longer conveyed the same meaning. Similarly, certain types of clothing are often worn to identify with a given culture or subculture.

Deuteronomy 22:5 reminds us of an important principle: The clothes we wear often reflect our inner attitudes. Clothes often are used to call attention to what we feel within. Clothes can communicate a message.

Consider the young people who wear torn blue jeans to church. They may have other clothes at home but prefer to show up with the most worn and torn pair they can find. By rejecting the accepted Sunday attire, they call attention to themselves and are silently asking, "Do you accept me for who I am or for the clothes I wear?" If they're asked to sit in the back row—if indeed they're permitted to sit at all—they have received the answer they suspected was coming, namely that they are unwelcome in their casual garb.

Arguments over such matters only compound the problem. The church must be willing to love all people, even those who dress to get attention. Such people are crying for acceptance, and it is our duty—our privilege—to accept them as Christ accepts us.

Clothes communicate attitudes. We can communicate by dressing poorly, extravagantly, or immodestly. In any apparel we wear, we may be reflecting our attitude to society around us.

## LIVING IN STYLE

In chapter two, we saw that a primary characteristic of worldliness is putting the wrong value on legitimate concerns. Clothing is necessary. But we can become a slave to new styles and fashions. Jesus taught that anxiety about clothing was characteristic of worldly attitudes (Matthew 6:25).

Today, this anxiety is expressed by a perpetual desire to be in style. Whether or not we realize it, we wear what the fashion designers decide we will wear.

Mass media, especially social media, has made us self-conscious. Woe unto those who are not squeezed into the mold! Clothing that looked so right five years ago looks so wrong today.

Harvey Cox, in *The Secular City*, scrutinizes the insecurity of our age. Changes take place so rapidly that no one can keep up with them. The insecure and anxious constantly read the latest magazines, look at the latest ads, and admire the latest public hero. According to Cox, this was one of the reasons for the success of *Playboy* magazine. The reader, Cox says, knows "the style will change and he must always be ready to adjust. His persistent anxiety that he may mix a drink incorrectly, enjoy a jazz group that is passe or wear last year's necktie style is comforted by an authoritative tone in Playboy beside which papal encyclicals sound irresolute."[1]

Cox continues, "Those liberated by technology and increased prosperity to new worlds of leisure now become the anxious slaves of dictatorial tastemakers...*Playboy* mediates the Word of the most high into one section of the consumer world, but it is a word of bondage, not of freedom."[2]

All of us can succumb to the anxiety for the latest styles. Clothes can be used to protect our façade. Some men go to church to display the suits they couldn't conveniently wear during the week. Women have been known to skip a banquet or reject a wedding invitation because "I have nothing to wear," which more accurately stated is, "I have nothing *new* to wear." Unfortunately, attending church often means little more than joining the fashion parade.

In their constant quest for new fads, designers often resurrect the styles of twenty years ago. Since styles are based purely on conventional acceptance, Charles Spurgeon aptly defined fashion as "the collective opinion of fools."

Of course, new styles are not sinful. Neither is there anything inherently spiritual about adopting styles five years late. But anxiety about whether we are wearing the latest fashions indicates that our security is misplaced.

There is no virtue in old fashions, but apart from social acceptance, there is no virtue in the new ones either. We can influence our friends by the way we dress, but God remains unimpressed.

Since styles vary from culture to culture and year to year, should Christians have standards in matters of dress? Do schools have a right to demand dress codes? If so, how can lines be drawn?

## DRAWING THAT INVISIBLE LINE

In a logic class I took back in university, our instructor explained six logical fallacies. One was entitled, "The Argument of the Beard." Briefly, our assignment was to decide how many hairs constitute a beard. Two? Hardly. Fifty? It's doubtful. Four hundred? Perhaps. But what about

399 or 398? How do you know when you've crossed the line? Answer: You don't. Obviously, there is no way to settle the question as to how many hairs are needed to make a beard. Someone else could always suggest one more or one less. And there would be no way to prove which arbitrary choice is right.

Now let us suppose a president of a company insisted that his manager hire only men with beards. Could the manager carry out such instructions? Or would the manager have to say, "Since we have no authoritative way to distinguish between someone who has a beard and one who does not, we cannot grant the president's request"? Sound a bit silly?

If we follow this reasoning to its logical conclusion, it leads to absurdity. We would end up being unwilling to classify anyone as either having a beard or not having one, simply because we don't know where to draw the line. But obviously there is a great difference between a few whiskers and a beard; there is even a significant difference between someone with a full beard and someone with a goatee, even though we cannot decide precisely when one becomes the other.

The point the professor was trying to make is that although there is no exact way to distinguish between someone who has a beard and someone who does not, it's wrong to assume we can't recognize significant differences between them. To put it another way, important differences may exist between two quite similar entities, even though we can't easily pinpoint where they differ. We must draw lines even where fine distinctions are involved, even when our lines have to be quite arbitrary. It's simply not true that we should consider two things as equal because a distinction between them may be difficult to make.

This is why censorship usually fails in our free society. One group of judges may decide to draw the line at one point; others may choose another. But no one can say authoritatively where art ends and pornography begins. Can it be defined in terms of the amount of clothes or lack of them worn by the model? Why is one pose suggestive and another not? Add to this the fact that one picture affects each individual differently (depending on their background, taboos, or lifestyle), and any distinctions dissolve into an undifferentiated blur. Consequently, pornography peddlers insist that all types of books and movies should be permissible simply because no one can define pornography with precision. So in the absence of authoritative guidelines, our society is accepting all types of reading and viewing material without raising an eyebrow.

Such reasoning is ridiculous. Just as a great difference exists between a full beard and a half-dozen whiskers, a vast difference exists between pornography and *Time* magazine. There is also a difference between one suggestive scene and an X-rated movie. It still remains necessary to decide what pornography is and what it is not, what is decent and what is indecent, even in situations where the issues are not altogether clear. And usually, it's much easier to draw the line than some of our modern hedonists would like us to believe. There may be some differences of opinion, but that doesn't mean we are justified in accepting all types of art, movies, and literature. Briefly, the difficulty with making fine distinctions should not lead us to believe everything can be classified as being on the same level. We must be willing to draw lines personally and *corporately*.

The same principle applies to making other types of rules as well. Parents are constantly faced with the decision of making rules for their children; Christian schools often revise their handbooks. Questions arise regarding hairstyles, dress codes, and personal conduct. Sometimes making such rules necessitates arbitrary distinctions. Yet such distinctions must be made.

Imagine a continuum between 1 and 100. Suppose 1 represents an extremely strict, rigid lifestyle. Let 100 represent permissive and irresponsible conduct. All of the other numbers represent varying types of lifestyles, progressing steadily from the most strict (1) to the most permissive (100). Now imagine that parents decide to give their children freedom up to 30. Admittedly, the choice is arbitrary, since there is no great difference between 30 and

31. But they have to draw the line somewhere. Perhaps next year they will tighten the requirements, choosing 25; or they may become more lenient and choose 35. Just because there may be latitude for change—even disagreement—does not mean that parents and schools should permit all styles of conduct because they can't decide with absolute certainty where to draw the line.

Decide they must! For if they don't make a stopping point somewhere on the continuum, some people would choose level of conduct at 100 and be ruined in the process.

Can we draw the line in matters where the issues are not entirely clear? Yes. We can't allow the difficulty of making precise distinctions frighten us into making no distinctions at all! We need the wisdom of God in knowing how to strike a balance between severe restrictions, that would deny believers legitimate pleasures, and an atmosphere of leniency, that would permit all types of conduct under the guise of Christian liberty.

## SUITABLE MODESTY

Let's apply this principle to the question of modest clothing. Years ago, a designer of enticing women's apparel candidly remarked that fashions were purposely abbreviated "because a woman should be just as seductive in the daytime as she is at night." Swimsuits have been trimmed to the least possible coverage in order to accentuate sexual attraction.

Those who wear less appealing clothes are labeled prudes.

Making distinctions in our permissive society is not easy. For example, at what point does a skirt become a miniskirt? Four inches above the knee? Three and a half? Such questions are technically unanswerable. There is no point measurable in inches or centimeters where modesty ends and immodesty begins. And for this reason, many have falsely concluded that it doesn't matter what they wear. Since no precise limits can be agreed upon, all forms of dress have been assumed to be on the same level. But they aren't!

Once again, while no one can measure modesty with a yardstick, it may be necessary to choose a measurable requirement and adhere to it. Those who make such decisions are frequently accused of being arbitrary and of making petty distinctions. Certainly such a charge is sometimes justified, especially in matters where no biblical principle is involved. But in many instances fine distinctions are necessary. In fact, there are times when a rule can only be made arbitrarily. We must choose a certain point beyond which we—and those for whom we are responsible—cannot go.

Obviously there will be disagreements as to where lines should be drawn on specific issues. There will be differences from country to country and family to family. For example, modest apparel in the Far East may be different from modest apparel in the United States. Also the modesty of previous centuries (where elbows and ankles had to be covered) may not be the modesty of today. Usually when new forms of dress are introduced into a culture, they may be thought immodest until, after saturating the market for some time, they're not given a second thought or glance. This explains why Christians may shun certain styles at first and then accept them in the next generation. Such changes do not reflect unfavorably on the preceding generation, since standards of acceptance vary. Nor should we pride ourselves in being enlightened because we think we have overcome some of the hang-ups of the past. But we must remember that God's standards have not changed, even though we may have adopted new styles or changed some of our rules. Once again, we must be driven back to principles of purity, honesty, and consideration for others, which transcend all cultural gaps. We will have differences—choosing different points along the continuum—but we should avoid petty scruples. We should especially be careful to avoid dogmatism in matters where no moral issues are at stake.

Remember also that we must not exercise our freedom if it would hinder others in the Christian life. We should be willing to lay aside weights which might not only be a burden to us but to others as well. Let's not be quick to judge others who have drawn the line at a different point than we would. We may have weaknesses they don't; conversely, they may need restrictions we find unnecessary. Of course, we should understand that such flexibility applies only to areas where the moral and spiritual implications are unclear, and therefore, legitimate differences exist.

## CULTURAL ACCEPTANCE

What about instances where dress codes have nothing to do with modesty or immodesty but are purely matters of cultural acceptance? For example, here is a quotation from a Christian school's handbook: "Young men will wear shirts and ties to all classes and coats to the noon and evening meals. The student body will always dress appropriately and will adhere to standards that will please fundamental Christian parents across America."

Obviously sports coats and ties have nothing to do with modesty. Such restrictions have no scriptural basis. Does this mean such rules are unnecessary, irrelevant, or evil? Such standards are legitimate, as long as the faculty and students understand clearly that such conformity is not the result of any biblical principle but rather the result of social pressure from the evangelical (fundamental) community. These requirements are made for sociological reasons (pleasing the parents, status in the community, getting jobs, or being acceptable to certain churches). Such requirements are proper for the above reasons, but this should be clarified, lest such rules are considered synonymous with Christianity.

Many parents have discovered to their dismay that children can easily conform to the dress codes (and standards) of the church and yet reject their heritage when they come of age. Unfortunately, part of the reason this happens is because we have evaluated them outwardly and thought all was well because they appeared to conform to mores of the church or school. One of the most subtle pharisaical errors is to cleanse the outside of the cup (everyone probably was required to wear just the right robes) yet inwardly be filthy (Matthew 23:25). Christ's remark to them was, "First clean the inside of the cup and the plate, that the outside also may be clean" (v. 26). To put it in contemporary terms: Whenever we dress in our best clothes (suits and ties on Sunday), we had better know that this in no way means we are pleasing to God. The poor who have no suits and see no need for ties and come to church barefoot might well enter the kingdom of heaven ahead of us.

On the other hand, we should not be critical of those who happen to be in step with the fashions of the day. Parents have often unwisely forced their children to wear clothes of the past generation, thinking contemporary styles were sinful. This gives the erroneous impression that a Christian is one who is always ten years behind the times.

To be balanced, we should gladly accept new styles

which are purely cultural (and modest). Yet on the other hand, it's sinful to be obsessed with every present fad. Those who use clothing to enhance their social status have compromised with the world and are in danger of the pride of life.

In churches and schools, children and students should be reminded that they have an obligation to obey their parents and those in authority over them (Ephesians 6:1–2; 1 Timothy 5:17). So if restrictions are made, they should be obeyed, even when it seems such rules are unnecessary. Part of the way we learn discipline is to obey those over us in the Lord, even when they may be wrong. And we should not merely obey outwardly but have a corresponding attitude of obedience as well.

In short, it may be necessary to dress according to certain restrictions, even when biblical principles are not at stake. The reason for such rules are, however, purely cultural and are for the purpose of social acceptance.

## PERSONAL APPLICATIONS

We are confronted daily with the need to make personal decisions. Our appearance reflects, in part, our relationship with the world. When the apostle Peter was discussing the conduct of women—especially those women whose husbands were not Christians—he said the husbands would be won by the behavior of the wives. Then he added, "Do not let your adorning be external—the braiding of hair and the putting on of gold jewelry, or the clothing you wear—but let your adorning be the hidden person of the heart with the imperishable beauty of a gentle and quiet spirit, which in God's sight is very precious" (1 Peter 3:3–4).

Although this is addressed to women, the principle applies to us all: Our inner attitude is more important than the beauty of clothes. To be adorned outwardly and yet be sinful inwardly is hypocrisy. Cleansing the outside of the cup but being filthy inside is scarcely a new ploy.

There is a related principle here as well: Clothes should not be used to draw attention away from the enduring qualities of godliness. Perhaps this is what Paul had in mind when he wrote, "Women should adorn themselves in respectable apparel, with modesty and self-control, not with braided hair and gold or pearls or costly attire" (1 Timothy 2:9).

Those who dress to impress others or to flaunt their physique have capitulated to the attitude of the world.

We've come a long way from fig leaves, but, as yet, we have not escaped the consequences of our sinful environment. The fact that we are a part of our cultural heritage is not in itself a cause for alarm, except when that culture deviates from the standards of Scripture.

There will always be borderline cases; the issues will often be blurred. It is then that we need to know what is right, what is wrong, and how to draw a line between the two. Doing that necessitates God's wisdom. Blessed are they to whom such is given!

## QUESTIONS FOR DISCUSSION

1. Why is modesty a necessity?
2. What happens when we seek "freedom" by way of permissiveness?
3. Read Deuteronomy 22:5 and 1 Corinthians 11:14–15. Why are gender-neutral trends morally significant?
4. What should be our attitude toward clothing? What is significant about the way we dress?
5. Discuss the logical fallacy "The Argument of the Beard." Show why it is important we draw the line in matters when the issues are not entirely clear.
6. Distinguish between biblical principles and social pressure. Using Matthew 23:25–26, Ephesians 6:1–2, and 1 Timothy 5:17, discuss the balance we must achieve.

ERWIN W. LUTZER

CHAPTER TEN

# GUARD YOUR HEART

Imagine living in a city where you're repeatedly attacked by your enemies. Wouldn't you construct defenses for you and your family's protection? The book of Proverbs describes the dangers of letting down our guard, "A man without self-control is like a city broken into and left without walls" (25:28). We are in a fierce battle for our souls, opposed by agendas and ideologies outside the home. But perhaps the potential danger is even greater from forces within our homes, reaching us through our computers, televisions, tablets, and smart phones.

Do you have walls to keep the enemy out? Do you have the self-control to guard your heart?

Many questions surround our usage of media and technology today: How much entertainment should we let into our home? How much of the media are we able to tolerate? How are new technologies shaping our hearts?

Of course, we are very thankful for technology, and all

the ways it has improved our lives. But here is a caution: Media is not neutral. Built into many of the engines of technology are hidden values coming at us through our devices. Though smartphones had their beginning in the late 1990s, it was the advent of the Apple iPhone in 2007 when smartphones, as we think of them today, became available to the masses. A few years later, the Barna Group reported in their 2013 study, *The Changing Shape of Temptation*, that about half of Americans (44%) admitted to spending too much time consuming media. Most Americans (59%) said they don't attempt to avoid temptations surrounding media. When asked why they thought people gave into temptations of any sort, 50% indicated they didn't know, while 20% said temptation is a means of escape. Another 20% said they enjoy it. But only 1% said that people give in to temptation because of their sinful nature. Isn't it a wonder? The human soul is incapable of properly assessing its true condition.[1]

In this chapter, we'll explore the myths surrounding media engagement, certain tests to filter our media consumption, and the imperatives Christians must be aware of as we live *in* the world of media, but not *of* it. Let's first dispel three myths that all of us have accepted at one time or another.

## THE THREE MYTHS

**Myth 1:** *Technology is totally neutral.* Some would suggest technology itself is neutral, with its ethics grounded in how we use it. Not quite! As Neil Postman said, "Every technology has an inherent bias....Only those who know nothing of the history of technology believe that a technology is entirely neutral....Each technology has an agenda of its own."[2] Don't kid yourself. The medium is not neutral.

Think about it. Why are billions of dollars spent on advertising today if what we see doesn't affect what we do? Marketers know we are desire-driven. If we see it often enough, soon we're buying it. We scroll through and watch limitless content every day. Language is used and misused to create reality. In an era of instant access to bite-sized news and propaganda on the internet, misinformation spreads fast. Perhaps most alarming is that teens are more connected than ever in this digital age through social media. A Pew study in 2022 found about 46% of American teens are online "almost constantly." Some 54% of US teens say it would be very hard or somewhat hard for them to give up social media.[3] Even teenagers are acknowledging the challenges of being constantly online and on social media.

Unlike public or cable television, many subscription-based video streaming services offer an autoplay function. A number of movies or shows are automatically queued up, ready for you to binge watch, one right after another. The stream no longer stops or pauses for a commercial, allowing you to watch for hours on end, without interruption.

The gamification of our culture, as well as search engine algorithms, reward addictive behavior. Now I know there are some creative and helpful video games. My own grandchildren have played some, which were carefully chosen by their parents. Nevertheless, there's no doubt immersive online worlds are part of daily living (and not just for children), with implications for our health, privacy, and human interactions. Many parents are not engaged with their teen's usage of media, or if they are, they're uncertain of how to navigate the influx of media in their homes. More on that later.

**Myth 2:** *What I watch doesn't affect me.* Have you believed that lie? What we watch, listen to, and browse, does affect us, whether consciously or subconsciously. The media filling our homes is saturated with explicit content. In a report by Common Sense Media, 15% of teens surveyed said they first saw online pornography at or before the age of 10. Most teens, 58%, have accidentally seen pornography, while 44% of teens look for it intentionally.[4] You can't go online, look at the news, or visit social media without provocative images or explicit click-bait popping up.

The medium of technology is biased against a life of holiness and commitment. It is bent against purity of life and thought. The point is, we *are* affected.

Remember what the Bible says, "For as he thinks within himself, so he is" (Proverbs 23:7, NASB). Christians must be aware of the influence their technology and media usage has on both their minds and bodies. What we see influences what we think and what we desire. That is the real you.

**Myth 3:** *With some basic guidelines, we can use technology for our good.* This is true in one sense but it is misleading. In a culture with a relative view of truth, what is our standard? Christians must navigate the rapid changes in technology with the authority of God's Word. Most business owners could not possibly operate without media and technology. In fact, with the medium of digital currency, we are quickly moving towards a cashless society. In building an ethic of digital money, have we considered biblical principles?

Christians at the forefront of developing technologies need to make crucial moral decisions while continuing to grow in their discernment as disciples of Christ. As we discussed in previous chapters about money, biblical principles also apply to technology: generosity, stewardship, and dependence on God in every aspect of our lives. Submission to God's ultimate authority is the only way to have a moral compass amid the shifting waters of technology.

I would rather stand on a bridge, trying to convince the Mississippi River to flow the other way, than attempt to change someone who is absolutely content with their media consumption, compulsion, or addiction. I'm convinced that if we're going to be free of these kinds of addictions, attractions, pressures, and cravings, true life change must start with prayer and fasting, coming from a posture of yieldedness to God. If we're going to use technology for the glory of God, the whole network of technologies that are against us and against Christian living must be redeemed.

Amid the rising tide of media and technology, we might acknowledge the media's effect on our lives and souls, but ultimately, only God can free our hearts from our addictions and habits. In a world of pornography, addiction, and distraction, only God can change the hearts and lives of people. I believe that with a concerted, prayerful investigation of our lives by the Holy Spirit, there is going to be victory. With man it is impossible but with God all things are possible.

## THE THREE TESTS

So the question before us is this: How do we redeem media and technology for the glory of God? In our individual, personal, and private use of the media, how do we evaluate the content and the technology behind it?

Let's be specific. We must have a strategy to test the positive and negative potential of these devices and media platforms. As I already mentioned in chapter seven, the

Scripture's timeless truths can be applied in any context, directly to our hearts. Here are three applicable tests:

**The Content Test.** Does this fuel the lust of the eyes, the lust of the flesh, and the pride of life in me? (see 1 John 2:16). We might immediately think of the detrimental effect of degrading movies, which are out of bounds for believers. But let's also consider music that technology can either enable us to create or listen to. The Scriptures give certain tests as to what content and direction songs and music should have. Songs can be used to worship God (Ephesians 5:18–19; Colossians 3:16–17); edify one another (1 Corinthians 14:26); and edify God's people, "Making melody to the Lord with your heart" (Ephesians 5:19).

What part should music have in our lives? It was created by God to aid us in our worship and edification. Music appeals to our sense of harmony and artistic beauty. While we might appreciate music's beauty, a song's message, or a musician's skill, the ultimate purpose, according to Scripture, is to enrich our worship of God and to increase spiritual edification. But like everything else that humans touch, it can become twisted and corrupted. Music should not drive our sexual impulses or increase our appetite for violence. Any music which normalizes our love for the world system will break down our moral resistance. Any content must be judged according to a high biblical standard.

**The Control Test.** Am I able to practice self-control in this? Paul says in 1 Corinthians 6:12, "'All things are lawful for me,' but not all things are helpful. 'All things are lawful for me,' but I will not be dominated by anything." After we pass the content test, the question remains, "Does it control me?" "It" can be anything: a smartphone, a social media site, a game, music, or video steaming. For those things which may be lawful or even quite innocent, are you controlling them or are they controlling you?

The way to find out whether you are in charge is simply this: Decide to quit whatever it is for a week or two to see if you can. When I go for three consecutive days without media, there is free time, and silence to hear God's voice. Do you end your day with social media or with reading the Scriptures? Do you reach for your device first thing in the morning or your Bible? Start and end your day with Scripture—and the peace of God in your mind and heart. Don't let technology shape who you become.

Years ago, while visiting a local mall, I noticed a little boy, about two years old, sobbing in a shopping cart. In his little hands, he held tightly to a toy steering wheel, turning it to the right with all he had. But the cart turned to the left because his mother was the one in charge. His steering wheel wasn't connected to anything that mattered. Do you *believe* you're in control of a particular technology? If you can't go without it for a week or two, you'll discover that you are not in charge at all. It's only the illusion of being in charge. Technology is meant to be a tool, not a slave master. Anything—a person, an institution, an image, a social media platform, or a pleasure—that is substituting for the place of God in our lives, is our master. In fact, it's become an idol.

**The Clock Test.** Is this investment of my time redemptive? In Ephesians 5:16–17, we are called to make "the best use of the time, because the days are evil. Therefore do not be foolish, but understand what the will of the Lord is." The imagery Paul depicts with "making the best use of" is to buy back or redeem the time, because we have multiple pressures on our time. We can buy back or redeem time for God by serving, worshiping, and praising Him, as well as studying His Word, instead of submitting to the pressures technology brings into our lives.

Let's suppose you watch videos for two hours a day. That's 730 hours a year. If you begin to multiply it by ten, you arrive at around 7,300. So 7,300 hours (or about ten months) over ten years is quite an investment of time just watching videos every day. What's your return on investment? Does it make you more Christlike? Are you walking more closely with God?

## THE FIVE IMPERITIVES

As we daily evaluate our media and technology use with these three tests, what must we do when we're tempted to touch technology or watch and listen to content that are not honor the Lord? Here are five imperatives we must live by to find victory in saying "No!" to those impulses.

**1. Recognize the battle.** We must recognize the spiritual nature of the conflict. "For we do not wrestle against flesh and blood, but against the rulers, against the authorities, against the cosmic powers over this present darkness, against the spiritual forces of evil in the heavenly places" (Ephesians 6:12). I still vividly recall the day when Rebecca and I logged into our first in-home internet provider: America Online (AOL). That night I had what I would describe as a demonic dream. It was horrific. In my dream, three evil spirits had me up in a corner. I felt totally and completely helpless. I had no power to fight them.

Can you imagine how relieved I was when I woke up from that nightmare? I believe that dream was God's gracious gift to me, helping me realize, "You now have something in your home that Satan wants to use to destroy you." Even now, if I am ever tempted to scroll, type, or visit websites I shouldn't, I remember the dream. And now I warn you: Satan wants to use those smartphones and computers and other technologies to destroy you. There are millions who are bound by pornography, addicted to violence, and killing their integrity in anonymity. Don't go there. Let me repeat: don't go there!

Don't lose heart; Jesus has prayed for you: "I do not

ask that you take them out of the world, but that you keep them from the evil one" (John 17:15).

**2. Respond to the battle.** We must commit to God's cleansing work. How do we respond to the spiritual warfare surrounding media and technology? The book of James gives us clear guidance to submit to God, resist the devil, and confess our sin (4:7–10).

First, *we submit completely.* As you get up in the morning, submit to God as an act of worship. Invite God's presence into your life with a prayer such as, "God, my life is Yours. All that I am is Yours. I give You my day with all its emotions and the coming interruptions and challenges. I give You this day with gratitude and praise, and I receive Your promises from Your hand." Quote God's promises. Submit unconquered sin or habits to God. And the simple truth is this: God really does want to fight for you. When you draw near to Him; He'll draw near to you.

Second, *we resist continually.* I have an acquaintance who was addicted to pornography. While visiting in my backyard once, he said this, which I hope is branded on all our minds, "Once you go on that path, it will take you places you never thought you'd ever go." Resist the devil and he will flee from you. This was evident in Jesus' life. In the desert, Jesus resisted Satan's temptation and Satan left and waited for a more opportune time (Luke 4:13). Don't stop resisting. Quote Scripture. Declare, "I will not go into

Satan's territory. I resist him in the name of Jesus."

Finally, *we confess thoroughly*. Though we can't purify our own hearts, God can cleanse our conscience. We must completely confess every sin God brings to our attention. "He is faithful and just to forgive us our sins and to cleans us from all unrighteousness." (1 John 1:9) Many of you are forgiven, but are you cleansed? Cleansing is the subjective word by which we not only are declared forgiven because of Christ's work on our behalf, but we know in our hearts we are forgiven. Get specific as you agree with God about your sins, including those on your media consumption or misuse of technology. Only then are you ready to receive God's full and thorough cleansing. The heart of condemnation will be gone.

**3. Implement rules.** We must set media standards based on the principles of God's Word. Would you believe me if I told you thieves are invading your home? They're stealing your child's soul, or perhaps even yours. You still feed and clothe your child, but your child's soul—their heart— belongs elsewhere. Let's name the thieves! The television, the internet, the VR headset, the smartphone, and the tablet. The devices in your child's bedroom (or your own) may already be stealing your souls. Are your defenses up?

Rules and guidelines, based on these and other biblical principles, must be in each home. Yes, rules! Perhaps it's time you designated where in the house your family may use devices. Are bathrooms or bedrooms allowed or should it be restricted to the family room? Another rule to consider: No devices on at night; pick yours up in the morning. Finally, it's time to set up media filters. Even if the filter can be circumnavigated, at least it prevents us or our children from accidentally coming across explicit material.

What if your child says, "You don't trust me?" Here's the answer, "No, I don't." Why not? "Because I don't trust myself." It was Martin Luther who said, "I fear my own heart more than I do the pope." Do you know what's going on in the secret parts of your child's life and in their friend circle? Our hearts are so prone to wander. That's why we also need other believers.

**4. Build healthy relationships.** Have you surrounded yourself with other Christians? The best way to begin the process of overcoming addictions is healthy relationships with other people. Healthy relationships breed health. It gives us perspective according to God's Word. It gives an opportunity for us to share without fear of rejection or condemnation. Do you have an accountability partner? Are you talking with your child or teen regularly? Christian community will also help us meet the challenge of impacting our world for Christ. More on this in chapter 14.

**5. Practice spiritual disciplines.** Out of all these imperatives, this one depends on God's grace the most. As we spend regular times in prayer, Bible reading, confession, corporate worship, and so on, we begin to love what God loves. Christianity is different from all the other religions of the world at this point. They all say that we should love one another out of a sense of duty. Christianity says you love because you've already been loved by God (1 John 4:19). Before you open the app, visit the webpage, or turn on the power button, concentrate on God's promises and the Scriptures you've memorized. A man I was counseling memorized Scripture. Then, when faced with a significant temptation, he was not only able to walk away, but did so with a great sense of peace.

Some might ask, "Is practicing spiritual disciplines legalistic?" As we discussed in chapter seven, of the three major forms of legalism, the danger in them all is *self-righteousness.* A list cannot define sinful activities but it can provide limitations; Christians live by principles.

Are you willing to ask God what it will take to live this out, giving up any types of addictions or compulsions? The purpose would be to develop the fruits of the Spirit, including self-control.

## CONCLUSION

Today our society is mad, driven with a mirage of pleasure. Of course we can't live without engaging with some form of technology. In this chapter, we've distinguished between its value and its detriment of temptation and seduction.

Every heart loves something. The Bible is very clear: we are desire-driven. Whichever is the greatest desire wins. Our desire should be for another Kingdom, and for another King. The deeper we are into the world's system, the more difficult the struggle. But it is a winnable war because Jesus died that we might be free from the effects and the power of the world. Even if you feel powerless or defenseless, do whatever God has asked you to do. We are fighting for our souls and for our families. We are training for another world.

*"My son, be attentive to my words; incline your ear to my sayings. Let them not escape from your sight; keep them within your heart. For they are life to those who find them, and healing to all their flesh. Keep your heart with all vigilance, for from it flow the springs of life. Put away from you crooked speech, and put devious talk far from you. Let your eyes look directly forward, and your gaze be straight before you. Ponder the path of your feet; then all your ways will be sure. Do not swerve to the right or to the left; turn your foot away from evil."* —Proverbs 4:20–27

## QUESTIONS FOR DISCUSSION

1. From what perspectives must a Christian evaluate technology and media?
2. Discuss the origin and value of recent technology.

What does Scripture have to say regarding the goals and purposes of technology?

3. How effective is media, art, and technology as a means of communicating scriptural truth?

4. Discuss the dangers of becoming "addicted" to technology and the entertainment industry.

# PART III

# FINDING GOD'S DIRECTION
# IN THE WORLD'S CONFLICTS

ERWIN W. LUTZER

## CHAPTER ELEVEN

# THE TENSIONS OF DOCTRINE

When we love the people of the world but shun the world system, we are immediately involved in a curious conflict. We encounter a variety of pressures, all competing for our allegiance. For example, when we love people we'll be tempted to compromise our doctrine to accommodate those who have deviant or even heretical views.

As a reaction to such pressure, some orthodox churches believe doctrinal purity necessitates a form of isolationism from the moral and spiritual milieu of our day. In extreme cases, some churches believe they have sole possession of the truth and only those who agree with them are the spiritual remnant of this age. Like Elijah, they are convinced that they alone have refused to bow the knee to Baal. But perhaps they, like the prophet also, have greatly underestimated the number of true prophets God has preserved.

On the other hand, some churches and individuals have become involved in directly penetrating the world and, in their enthusiasm, have neglected necessary doctrinal matters. As a result, their effectiveness has been weakened because their theology has been watered down.

Both extremes are to be avoided. Our love for the people of the world should not make us disregard doctrinal content; nor should we believe that only those who agree with us in every detail deserve our fellowship and support.

## DOCTRINAL SEPARATION

The Scriptures teach that doctrinal integrity must play a vital part in wholesome penetration of the world. This balance will rescue us from the sentimentalism which is willing to disregard doctrinal differences in the interest of serving love. On the other hand, doctrinal purity is not an excuse to be isolated from social, moral, and spiritual needs of our time. Nor does it necessitate a rigid conformity to every detail of a given doctrinal position.

Our love for one another and the world should not make us ignore doctrinal matters. We have all heard the plea, "If we could just set aside our doctrinal differences and show love and unity, we'd win the world to Christ." There is little doubt that petty doctrinal issues have often been blown out of proportion, and theological disagreements frequently give the world a distasteful picture of Christianity. Our disagreements cannot be ignored, but the way we handle them should be an example of love and Christian concern.

At what places must lines be clearly drawn? Love cannot tolerate organic unity with those whose fundamental views are distorted. Under the guise of love, evangelical churches have cooperated in evangelistic endeavors with liberal churches. Seminaries which were founded on the basis of orthodoxy have shifted to a position that denies the authority of Scripture. Those who have opposed such changes are often labeled "heresy hunters" or "belligerent." Presumably, love should cover a variety of doctrinal opinions. The argument that love should make us tolerant of all sorts of doctrinal perspectives is powerful, since it implies that orthodox churches are engaged in irrelevant hair-splitting while the needs of people are ignored.

How do we answer the charge that insisting on doctrinal and moral purity is contrary to the love we should have for all men? The answer is to understand the meaning of the word *love*. Love is not to be equated with sentimentality; nor is it synonymous with tolerance. We often get the impression that the lenient are loving and the strict are unloving, but this is not the teaching of the New Testament. Love cannot bend to doctrine, and right doctrine can never be achieved without love. This is why the phrase "dead orthodoxy" is essentially a contradiction. We cannot be dead and truly orthodox at the same time.

Significantly, the book of 2 John, which contains a stern warning to false teachers and instructs believers that heretics should neither be received nor greeted, anticipates the modern notion that intolerance is contrary to love. John defines love in a single sentence: "And this is love, that we walk according to his commandments" (2 John 6). In other words, love is defined as obedience to God's commands. If we censure false teachers and refrain from bidding them Godspeed, we are (contrary to popular opinion) exercising love. Of course, such action should not be taken with an attitude of vindictiveness or superiority. It is possible to be correct doctrinally and have the wrong attitude toward those who are in error. Some Christians seem to take delight in using a magnifying glass to find fault; others, equally orthodox, handle error with a concerned attitude of love. The scriptural balance is "speaking the truth in love" (Ephesians 4:15). This means we must not merely be correct theologically, but be correct emotionally as well. If we guard the doctrine of Christ from misrepresentation, and if we defend the faith delivered to the saints, we have done the will of God. And *that* is love.

An example of how love cannot be allowed to produce tolerance for sin or doctrinal impurity is found in the nature of God. Since God is love, He did not want the entire human race to be lost in hell. Yet, this didn't mean He could wipe our slate clean so His loving desire would be satisfied. He could not compromise His justice or His hatred of sin. Therefore, He provided a method of redemption whereby

He could maintain His justice and yet fulfill His loving will for mankind. Christ became the propitiation (satisfaction) for sin, so God the Father could be just and at the same time, declare sinners righteous (Romans 3:26). In this way, His attributes were not compromised. Love can never lead to tolerance for sin or heretical doctrine; nor can doctrine replace love.

Where should we draw the line? We must begin with the doctrine of Christ. Paul insisted that the trumpet of the gospel be sounded with clarity. Writing to the Galatians, who were tempted to follow those who distorted the doctrine of Christ (i.e., those adding works to the gospel of grace), Paul warned, "But even if we or an angel from heaven should preach to you a gospel contrary to the one we preached to you, let him be accursed" (Galatians 1:8). Then, lest the Galatians should think they didn't hear him correctly, the apostle repeats the same words in the next sentence. Paul wanted his readers to understand that there were not two versions of the gospel; the gospel the Galatians began to follow was not another gospel or revelation from God: there was only one version of the gospel message. This verse alone should be sufficient to guard us from thinking that everyone who "proclaims Christ" is to be accepted without further reservations. We must make certain the content of the message is accurate. Is Christ preached as the one whose merit alone is sufficient for salvation, or is

He merely our example to which we must add our good works for salvation? Without specific content, the name *Christ* can be used (or rather, misused) to encompass any ideology, heresy, or pet project anyone might happen to choose. In our day, the banner of love is used to tolerate a broad spectrum of "other gospels." Paul reminds us that if someone does not proclaim the gospel of Christ as revealed in the Scriptures, such an individual is to be shunned.

The apostle John taught the same truth in equally vivid terms. He wrote that those who do not acknowledge Jesus Christ as coming in the flesh are deceivers and antichrists. Teachers who come to a church and do not bring the scriptural teaching of Christ should not be received into a home nor given a greeting, for such an encouragement makes the believer a participant in the false teacher's evil deeds (2 John 7–11). Added to these passages are extended sections in 2 Peter 2 and Jude's epistle, which are directed at false teachers. And though such apostates are sure to come into the church, believers should reject them and their heretical teachings. In a passage somewhat difficult to interpret, Jude teaches we should have mercy on those who pervert the teaching of Christ with an aim to fearfully snatch them out of the fire, making certain that we ourselves are undefiled (Jude 22–23). As taught in these and other passages, we cannot have unity with those who do not hold to the scriptural teaching of Christ. From such, we should separate ourselves.

It's popular to think churches would have a greater impact on the world if they were united organically. Not necessarily. Churches that have drifted from the deity of Jesus Christ and substitutionary atonement can have a greater social impact on the world if united; but union will not give them spiritual life. Someone has accurately observed that putting a group of graveyards together will not produce a resurrection. Evangelicals who turn to such churches for spiritual growth and an effective witness have turned from the living God to a dead corpse.

## FELLOWSHIP IN CHRIST

What about those who hold to a scriptural doctrine of Christ but do not believe in the inerrancy of Scripture? Or those whose eschatology (prophecy) is different from ours? Paul taught that all scriptural teachings were necessary (1 Timothy 4:11–16; 6:3–5; 2 Timothy 3:14–17). We should not conclude that other doctrines, such as eternal punishment (Matthew 25:46) or the trustworthiness of the Old Testament, are negotiable (Matthew 5:18). Even so, we can have fellowship with all those who are members of Christ's Body through faith in Him.

Yet we must realize we can have fellowship with others only to the extent that we are able to share a common life with them (which is the meaning of the word *fellowship*).

For example, we can have a certain type of fellowship with all people, since we share the common experience of life. But with those who don't understand the things of God, our fellowship is limited. The next level of fellowship is one we can have with all Christians. Regardless of doctrinal or denominational differences, all who have trusted Christ are a part of His body, and therefore, we can have meaningful fellowship with them. Also, our responsibility to Christians is greater than it is to the non-Christian world. Paul writes, "So then, as we have opportunity, let us do good to everyone, and especially to those who are of the household of faith" (Galatians 6:10). Then within the larger sphere of Christians, there are smaller circles of fellowship. It's in these particular groups where we are able to have the deepest level of mutual sharing, not merely because we have greater fellowship with those we know best, but also because we can have better fellowship with those who share our doctrinal views.

Those who believe in baptism by immersion wouldn't feel comfortable in a service where infant baptism took place. Yet both groups, who emphasize salvation through Jesus Christ alone and agree on other basic doctrines, can have truly beautiful fellowship despite their differences regarding the mode of baptism. We should not expect all Christians to agree regarding the interpretation of Scripture, nor should we expect blind conformity. We must be willing to allow for individual differences and, at the same time, recognize that other circles of fellowship exist.

Logically, we should choose a church whose doctrines correspond most closely to what we believe is taught in the Scriptures. And while we should love all others, we need not agree with them. In fact, we would not be true to our calling if we did.

Let's be specific. Suppose an evangelical seminary deviates from its original doctrinal position and teaches that the Scriptures are not inerrant but contain some historical and scientific blunders. At the same time, those who teach such errors might be men who display the fruit of the Spirit and are genuinely concerned about others. There's no question about their commitment to Christ. What should our response be? The most popular course of action is to let love (or what is thought to be love) rule. Those who may object to the school's position are usually accused of being divisive or obstinate or both. Misunderstandings develop, and each side is more convinced than ever to not budge. So the easy way out is to stop rocking the boat. In the interest of unity, we might let the matter rest.

Except for one fact. Many existing liberal schools began with a distinct Christian commitment. They began to slide when they started to question whether the Bible is completely trustworthy. They realized that if the Bible erred historically, there was no reason to believe it was reliable on spiritual matters either. A few generations later, it was just another book. Thus while individuals can sincerely love Jesus and yet deny inerrancy, a religious body cannot tolerate such a position indefinitely. The next generation will argue for more consistency, until an error is pushed to its logical conclusion.

Therefore, love will not tolerate such doctrinal deviation. *But love will attempt to resolve the disagreement in the right spirit and with transparent honesty.* Love will not distort the truth; nor will it seek self-glory; nor will it seek vindication. During times of disagreement, love will receive its ultimate test. If we love our fellow Christians when differences exist, this is surely a testimony to the supernatural power of Christ.

So the fact of disagreements regarding premillennialism, eternal security, and inspiration should be faced realistically and honestly. Such matters should not be ignored. But these differences provide an opportunity to display the love of Christ, not merely to those who agree with us but to those who disagree as well. We may be convinced a group of believers is in error; they might believe the same about us. As differences are discussed and defended, attitudes of humility and genuine concern should prevail.

Sometimes we are faced with the question of how we should respond to believers who are in liberal churches. Some have trusted in Christ alone for their salvation but have continued their ministry in denominational groups which have officially abandoned orthodoxy. Paul taught that we ought to separate ourselves from every believer who leads an unruly life, not according to the traditions which the apostles proclaimed (2 Thessalonians 3:6). Yet it is still possible that some are following the scriptural doctrines within the confines of a liberal denomination, even though we might feel they are disobeying the command to "go out from their midst, and be separate from them" (2 Corinthians 6:17). Perhaps we can't specify what our attitude should be in every case. Sometimes there are those who are proclaiming Christ clearly without compromise despite a given denominational label. Others (especially weak Christians) may not realize their group has compromised the Scriptures. So we must treat each case with wisdom, attempting to help others see the need for doctrinal purity and separation from those who have denied the faith.

A final word. We must make a distinction between personal fellowship and organic unity. The leader of a prominent evangelical organization told how he met a fellow believer in what can be confidently described as an apostate denomination. They put their arms around each other as brothers in Christ. Undoubtedly, this was a genuine expression of their mutual faith. But in publicizing that act, the impression was given (perhaps unwittingly) that we ought to open our eyes to the similarities we have with liberal groups rather than concentrate on our differences. Since God has His children everywhere, we should be willing to accept other groups (liberal or not) despite our doctrinal differences.

God has His children everywhere—even in unlikely places. And since they are a part of Christ's body, we should love them. But to conclude or even to give the impression that we can, on this basis, broaden fellowship or cooperation with liberal groups is false. Wherever we find a believer, we ought to rejoice. But because a liberal group happens to have a few believers, that fact should not make us more lenient towards teachings deviating from the basic facts of the gospel. Christ prayed that all who believed on Him would be one. But this unity is not the kind brought about by discarding differences or compromising doctrine. In Christ, we have a unity transcending the mere external act of outward organization or intellectual agreement. Christ's prayer has been answered because we are all members of His body. On a practical level, this unity can be displayed to the world by the way in which we handle our minor differences; we don't all have to believe the same on all points to achieve it. We can have marginal doctrinal differences and still cause the world to exclaim, "Behold how they love one another!" And that's something only a living God can enable us to achieve!

## QUESTIONS FOR DISCUSSION

1. How important are our doctrinal underpinnings? What two extremes are we to avoid?

2. How are we to maintain balance when doctrinal differences become an issue? Discuss the place of love in doctrinal opinions.

3. Read 2 John 6 and Ephesians 4:5. What guidelines must we exercise in our use of these verses?

4. Read Romans 3:26. On what doctrinal issue must we draw the line in our tolerance of other positions?

5. Define *fellowship*. Discuss the levels of fellowship we can experience with others. What determines our level of fellowship with others?

CHAPTER TWELVE

# GOD'S COMPASS POINTS UP

One of my classmates in college believed he was in love with two girls at the same time (perhaps a more welcome predicament for him than for the girls). How could he know which one (if either) he should marry? In church, he heard, "The will of God is found in the Bible." Initially, that sounded comforting, until he discovered that neither of the girls' names is mentioned in its pages.

A student sent his application to three colleges. He told the Lord he'd go to the one that accepted him. It sounded like a wise move, but, unfortunately, he was accepted by all three. "So now what do I do?" he blurted. A good question.

Living in this world demands that we make choices; not merely choices between good and evil but choices between two seemingly equal goods. If we're not careful, we might hastily conclude that the Bible isn't much help in making decisions where good and evil are not the real issues. Or else we can make the opposite mistake of trying to torture the Bible into giving us specific geographical guidance.

We've all heard stories about Christians who have been miraculously led by opening their Bible at random. I heard of one man who flopped his Bible open, and the first word he saw was *north*, so he set out to be a missionary in Alaska. I tried that once when I was in high school; I pointed my unguided finger at the strangest verses, but God's leading was as confusing as ever. It simply didn't work. But time doesn't wait for us. We must make choices.

Many of us look back with envy at the days of the Old Testament when God often spoke directly to men. Abram was called out of Ur of the Chaldees by a direct command of God. Gideon put out his fleece, and God used it to make His will clear. Now if we had directions like that, we would know precisely what to do; but in today's world, all the signals are confused, muddy, and blurred. There isn't much joy in going from pillar to post, hoping God will make the best of whatever we're doing. Is there a way out of the fog? Is it possible for a Christian to know God's will and enjoy doing it? Yes. And God wants that possibility to be a reality.

## THREE MISCONCEPTIONS

Unfortunately, some Christians think of the will of God almost solely in geographical terms (does God want me in Chicago or Atlanta?). But geographical questions are secondary, or more accurately, they're minor compared to the weightier matters of God's will. Choosing a country or locality is necessary and often frustrating, but such decisions will follow quite naturally once more basic questions have been clearly answered.

A second misconception of a host of Christians is that the will of God refers only to special vocations. So, God directs only missionaries, pastors, and other Christian workers (usually in that order), but His direction has no relationship to plumbers, factory workers, taxi drivers, and garbage collectors. Perhaps we're still living with the notion that washing dishes, digging ditches, and weeding a garden can never merit eternal reward. Only teaching a Sunday school class, witnessing, or preaching a sermon will receive honorable mention at the judgment seat. But in God's sight, our occupation is not nearly as significant as our motivation and obedience. Every Christian's employer is God, so whatever we do in the familiar routine of life should be done in His name (Colossians 3:17). Our attitude and faithfulness determine our reward.

It is true that those in vocational Christian work may have a distinct calling of God. To be a prophet in the Old Testament or a preacher in this age does demand special gifts and involves more responsibility than may be required for other vocations. For example, James warns, "Not many of you should become teachers, my brothers, for you know that we who teach will be judged with greater strictness" (3:1).

But even with these distinctions, every Christian, regardless of how famous their achievements, has an equal opportunity to please God by the faithful use of the gifts they have been given. On this basis, all members of the body of Christ stand on equal ground.

My point is this: Every Christian can have the satisfaction of doing God's will. There will be no second-class citizens at the judgment seat of Christ. The basis of judgment will be obedience to *what* God wanted us to do and *how* we did it. This evaluation will have little or no resemblance to our human standards of success.

A third misconception is that some consider the will of God to be so mysterious (now you see it, now you don't) they'll never know what His will is. And that, in turn, leads some to despair. The will of God, which is designed to be good, acceptable, and perfect, turns out to be frustrating and elusive. A deeply spiritual (though misinformed) missionary I know used to pray for special guidance about the most trivial matters. She would even try to decide whether it was God's will to wash her hair on a given evening. She was right in understanding that God is interested in the mundane affairs of life, but she was wrong in believing she always needed a special sign. Obviously, she was a mental wreck. She didn't realize that the will of God is simply living in obedience to whatever lies ahead. His guidance is not mysterious. In short, if your hair needs washing, wash it!

## AN ILLUSTRATION

God told Jonah to go to Nineveh. Unlike many of us, the prophet had the benefit of explicit instructions given to him by God Himself. He knew what he should do (preach) and he knew where to do it (Nineveh). But communication is not the most difficult problem God encounters when He directs us. A greater problem is our disobedience.

Evidently, Jonah decided to escape to Tarshish because he felt that Assyria would destroy Israel if Nineveh (its capital city) repented. So Jonah heroically risked his life in disobedience to God, hoping to spare God's chosen people. The decision seemed noble, but it was also sinful.

When he arrived at Joppa, he found a ship ready to leave for Tarshish. This coincidence probably confirmed his decision to disobey God's command. Perhaps he thought, *God has provided this ship, given me money to pay for the ticket, and there's room for one more. These circumstances are of God.* The first lesson we learn from Jonah is that a coincidence alone does not guarantee we've made a correct choice.

I heard a student say, "But I just happened to meet her. It was miraculous. My plane flight was canceled, so I stayed in Seattle a few days and we met. I'm sure our marriage is God's will." But Jonah reminds us that no set of circumstances or unusual events is confirmation of God's will—especially if we are violating a clear command. A

Christian who marries a non-Christian is out of God's will no matter how miraculously they met. A canceled plane flight doesn't necessarily confirm God's will. Nor does a feeling that "we get along so well together." *Nothing* can justify disobedience. Not even loving concern.

What happened to Jonah next? Did God abandon him? Since God's command to him had been so clear, it would have been reasonable for God to have said, "Jonah, I'm finished with you. I'll get someone else." But He didn't.

In fact, God went to a whole lot of trouble. Specifically, He (1) created a storm; (2) loaded the dice of the sailors so Jonah (rather than another man) was thrown into the sea; (3) appointed a great fish to swallow Jonah; (4) controlled the digestion of the fish so it vomited Jonah onto dry land. That's doing a lot for someone who was flagrantly disobedient. This leads us to a second observation: God is more concerned about keeping us in His will than we are to be kept in it! We often mistakenly get the impression that God expects us to walk such a fine line we're never sure we are in His will. And if we make one mistake, we think we might never get back onto the track. We believe that the will of God is a deep mystery God delights to hide from us. Only those with a high degree of spirituality have a chance of finding His elusive plan.

If God went through such pains to bring a prophet (who knew God's will clearly) back into His plan, think of what He will do for a Christian who wants to do the will of God but is temporarily confused as to what it is! God is well qualified to guide a willing heart.

Ponder this for a moment: Was Jonah in the will of God in the belly of the fish? The answer is no, for he had been scheduled to go to Nineveh. But because he disobeyed, God provided a special storm and a tailor-made fish to intercept His servant. In this secondary sense, Jonah was now in God's will: God manipulated circumstances and events so that Jonah ended up where God wanted him—in the belly of a fish.

God can take any situation—even our mistakes and failures—and make the best of it. Even our sins can be incorporated into His plan, so that all things work together for good. Of course this doesn't justify sin. There are serious consequences for disobedience. But God can use such experiences to teach us some needed lessons.

A girl came to me with a problem. "I've married the wrong man. I knew I shouldn't have done it. The only way out is divorce." Whether she married the "wrong one" or not, I can't say. But her attitude alone was sufficient to break up their marriage. Even if she had married the wrong man (a flimsy supposition), she failed to see that God could have used the relationship to work out His purposes. Of course, it might involve radical adjustments, suffering, and spiritual strain (since all disobedience has its price), but

God can indeed pick up the pieces and incorporate them into His plan.

The same can be said for those who are out of God's will geographically. One Christian *knew* God wanted him in Europe but ended up as a salesman in Canada. In later years, he wanted to go to Europe, but it was too late. He began a business at a service station and witnessed to everyone who came by. Two of his children became missionaries. He has lived a successful Christian life. Assuming that God did originally call him to Europe, is he in God's will now? Once again, we must say no; but because of God's goodness, we can say yes too!

God doesn't want us to live in the past! I have known Christians who have lived with deep regret because of a wrong choice made years before. They have come to Christ for forgiveness, but they're still plagued with guilt. They can trust Christ to forgive some sins but not all; the past is always with them. They have forgotten that the purpose of the cross is to repair the irreparable. A third lesson from Jonah: It is never too late to begin again; regardless of the past, we can be in the will of God *today*.

All of us make mistakes through ignorance or disobedience or both. But God never runs out of plans. He never says, "You blew it. You are not where I intended; I can't work you in anywhere else." God is never caught off guard. He has multiple contingency plans which He has already ordained to use. He will create fish, cause storms, and even use loaded dice to keep His children on the course.

## WHEN YOU MUST CHOOSE

Perhaps you felt uneasy about the story of Jonah. After all, he knew explicitly what God wanted him to do. How simple it would be if God were to speak to us directly, then we could be sure we were making wise decisions! I have good news for you: *He does!*

God's will is given to us verbally and directly. It is spelled out for us numerous times in the New Testament. For example, He wants us to put our trust in Christ (John 6:28–29); to give ourselves as a living sacrifice (Romans 12:1–2); not to try to please men but to please Him (Ephesians 6:5–6); and to give thanks in everything (1 Thessalonians 5:18). *This* is the will of God.

"But" someone says, "we've already agreed that the Bible doesn't specify who we are to marry, what our vocation should be, and where we should live." True. But *obedience to revealed truth guarantees guidance in matters unrevealed*. If we submit to the will of God as we read it in His Word, God is obligated (because of His promises) to guide us vocationally and geographically. There is a direct connection between our obedience to the commands of Scripture and God's guidance in the often unclear choices of everyday life.

David tells us about this relationship in Psalm 32. He describes his distress before he confessed his sin (vv. 3–4). After confession, he breaks out in praise to God and is assured of the promise, "I will instruct you and teach you in the way you should go; I will counsel you with my eye upon you" (v. 8). The assurance of God's guidance came when David cleansed his life from sin. The next verse cautions, "Be not like a horse or a mule, without understanding, which must be curbed with bit and bridle, or it will not stay near you." We thwart God's guidance by unconfessed sin; it is restored by confession.

Romans 12:1–2 makes a similar point. Giving our bodies as a living sacrifice and refusing to be conformed to this world is the prerequisite to proving what is the good, acceptable, and perfect will of God. As in the life of Jonah, the greatest obstacle to guidance is our disobedience or resistance to what God requires. I have known Bible school students who skipped missionary prayer meetings for fear they might be "called" to Africa. Some Christians are unwilling to give God their futures because they're convinced God will not give them a partner.

Often we're tempted to make choices on the basis of a worldly scale of values. We choose homes, cars, and vocations solely for prestige. When this happens, we lose a conscious sense of doing everything as unto God and not unto man. Like David, we have no assurance of God's guidance.

God's will for us is just as specific as the command given to Jonah, although its *content* is different. God's compass doesn't spin in a variety of confusing directions. He does not delight in our frustration when three possibilities open up before us, except, of course, when such frustration drives us to Him. His compass points upward, to Himself; our vertical relationship with Him is more important than the horizontal (worldly) decisions we face every day. That is why Christ promised that if we seek first God's kingdom and His righteousness, the needs of life would be supplied.

How does God direct us? Not with a blinding light from heaven nor a verse of Scripture selected at random. We commit our way unto Him and do whatever lies at hand, and He will control circumstances, change our inclinations, and lead us into opportunities which will be part of the divine plan. Also, He leads us to people who have the wisdom to give us counsel.

Do you feel inclined to be a missionary or minister of the gospel? Earnestly pursue the matter with prayer and guidance from trusted believers, and if your inclination is wrong, God will reveal it to you. Do you have three colleges you could attend? Be willing to go to any one of them, then select the one that seems to fit best with your pocketbook, interests, and location. If you have committed your way to God, He will stop you from making a wrong choice. Maybe He'll make you uneasy about one school or close the door to another. He has an unlimited number of ways to lead us. Relax. Commit your way to Him. God has no difficulty in guiding a willing and obedient servant.

God's will is good, acceptable, and perfect. We need not fear it. Once we are willing to do whatever He wants and to live in light of biblical commands, we step out in faith. He will intercept us when we make a mistake. Of course, if we are disobedient to the Scriptures, we will be disciplined. It might take a storm, a fish, and a desperate prayer, but He will be willing to redirect our steps.

God has a great investment in every Christian. He's interested in every detail of our lives. He wants us to make the small decisions as well as the big ones in dependence upon Him. This takes more faith than if He were to direct us visibly. Anyone can follow a blinding light; it takes greater faith to trust solely in God's promises. Make your decisions today by remembering that God places more emphasis on the spiritual than the geographical. Once we have settled our basic attitude toward Him (willing obedience), He has promised to take it from there. To put it concisely, "Trust in the LORD with all your heart, and do not lean on your own understanding. In all your ways acknowledge him, and he will make straight your paths" (Proverbs 3:5–6).

God did a lot for a disobedient prophet. He won't do less for an obedient servant. Remember, the compass points up.

## QUESTIONS FOR DISCUSSION

1. What three common misconceptions do Christians often have about the will of God?

2. Read the book of Jonah. Discuss how God worked out His will in the life of Jonah. What basic lessons can we learn from Jonah's experience?

3. Read John 6:28–29, Romans 12:1–2, Ephesians 6:5–6, and 1 Thessalonians 5:18. What can we learn about the will of God from these Scriptures?

4. Discuss this statement: "Obedience to revealed truth guarantees guidance in matters unrevealed."

5. What should be our basic attitude toward God in matters of His will for us.

ERWIN W. LUTZER

CHAPTER THIRTEEN

# THE AXE PUT TO THE ROOT OF THE TREE

I met a girl named Karen at a youth retreat. "I need some help because my life is a bit messed up," she modestly admitted. She was experiencing continual failure in her Christian life. Specifically, she told me she had five problems: sexual looseness, drinking, smoking, swearing, and bitterness against her parents. She stared defiantly into space wondering what to say next. I must admit I wasn't fully prepared for her next remark. In tears she added, "I'll have you know that I've come to Christ ten times with these problems, and He hasn't helped me a bit." Ten times she had come to the One who claimed to deliver people from their sins. But for Karen it hadn't worked.

There are hundreds of people like Karen trying to live the Christian life. As they become older, they eventually outgrow some of the sins of their youth, but their life remains as empty as before. The pleasures of youth give way to the desire for status; bitterness toward their parents leads to bitterness against their marriage partner; the habits which were practiced just for kicks in their youth have now ensnared them. Their sins may not be as obvious, but their defeat is just as real. Like Karen, they too have stood in a dedication service to sing, "I Surrender All," but it has not helped much, at least not for long.

At one time or another, everyone has felt like Karen did. I have. On the one hand, I have read of God's power; on the other hand, I have seen the failures in my life and wondered where the breakdown between the two occurs. One of the most practical questions we all face is how to translate God's promises into spiritual victory and personal fulfillment.

A minister's wife admitted candidly, "Ministers often leave a church essentially as they found it. They come and go, but the lives of the people remain the same. Those who sought status, money, or personal pleasure haven't changed even after years of sermons." Unfortunately, this woman spoke the truth. Spiritual growth cannot be measured with a yardstick, but we can't escape the suspicion that many who are exposed to biblical truth are not being changed by it. Why?

One reason is that we often adjust the outer fringes of our life to conform to the truth we hear. For example, when we are reminded we should read and study the Scriptures, we may become convicted and begin to meditate on the Word. But two weeks later, our determination has waned, and we lapse back into our former ways. Once again, we can go for days without reading the Bible or saying more than a routine prayer. Later, we may be challenged to witness, and we begin to share our faith. But this too lasts only for a time. We can follow this pattern for years and make little progress, simply because the core of our motivation and basic goals has remained the same despite minor adjustments.

It's also easy to become immune to truth. We don't believe the ads on television, and so we view the biblical promises with the same suspicion. We begin to believe (perhaps rightly so) there is very little said that we haven't heard before. Like Karen, we've tried it but it hasn't worked.

At other times, we may not even be aware we are out of step with Christ. The philosopher Descartes reminded us that it's possible to be asleep while dreaming we are awake, perhaps like the minister who dreamed he was preaching and then woke up and found out he was! The people of Laodicea thought they were in need of nothing but did *not know* they were wretched, pitiable, poor, blind, and naked (Revelation 3:17). We can be asleep spiritually yet be convinced we are wide awake. In such instances, only a tragedy or sudden emergency can bring us to our senses. Then we are forced to evaluate our priorities.

These are the symptoms, but is there a cure? Is there hope for Karen? For you? For me?

## THE STRUGGLE OF THE WILL

When Jesus was on Earth, did He do what He *wanted* to do? Yes. And no. Jesus had a passion to do the will of His Father. The prospect of being nailed to a cross outside the walls of Jerusalem was not glamorous. The Father's blueprint called for a shameful death, but Jesus didn't quibble over the plan. He was obedient to the point of death (Philippians 2:8) and could say with the psalmist, "I delight to do your will, O my God" (Psalm 40:8). Christ's only concern was the Father's will.

Yet we must see Christ's commitment from another perspective. Paul wrote, "For Christ did not please himself" (Romans 15:3). This doesn't mean Jesus was displeased with the Father's will, but rather that He was willing to set aside all personal considerations to finish the assignment He had been given. To put it another way, Jesus didn't ask, "What pleases Me?" but, "What pleases the Father?" And if the Father was pleased, the Son was pleased. The will of God was *all* that mattered. And Jesus is our model of commitment.

Whenever we're faced with a crucial decision, the world has taught us to ask, "What's in it for me? Will it give me pleasure? Profit? Security? Fulfillment? We aren't necessarily opposed to God; we just fit Him in wherever He is able to help *us*. The idea that our wills should be subjected to His control, even when our personal ambitions are at stake, isn't easy to accept. We can assent mentally to God's control, but in practice, we might still spend our lives pleasing ourselves.

How do we begin to let God be in control? We must give Him our bodies—our mind, talents, sex drive, and reputation. We (our total self) must be given to Him in a conscious act of commitment. This is difficult, so difficult that we will use any excuse to avoid the implications of such an act.

This is why Karen was not able to live a joyful Christian life, even though she had "come to Christ ten times." I asked if she would be willing to give herself to God so He could actually change her desires, dissolve the bitterness, and simply take charge. She considered the implications of this and then answered thoughtfully, "I don't want to forgive my parents. I have a right to be bitter." I explained that commitment meant more than forgiving her parents. God should have control over her future. She would have to recognize that He might lead her to become a missionary, or perhaps she would remain unmarried. But in return for letting God be in charge, she would be rewarded with a sense of fulfillment, victory, and peace. Her response was enlightening. "I expected you to simply pray for me," she explained. "If I have to give myself to God completely, if it means submitting myself to Him in the sense you mean, I'm not prepared for that." Karen left with her five problems. She had indeed come to Christ nearly a dozen times; she had come because she thought He'd help her stay out of trouble while she was pursuing her own desires. But when it came down to the moment of truth, she backed off. Giving ourselves to God is not easy.

Let's take our reputation as another example of continual struggle. On a plane, I met a man who was the director of a Christian organization. He told me about the pressure he faced in traveling from city to city. By virtue of his position, people had high expectations of him, and he had to make certain never to disappoint them. So he had to maintain his reputation. He was bound by the approval of men. The joy of his salvation was gone. He was not a free man.

Consider the minister who is relieved to discover church attendance was down during his vacation; he rejoices that the people respond to his ministry with more enthusiasm than they do for someone else. He isn't able to thank God for those who have gifts that are greater than his.

Then there are parents who are constantly protecting their reputation. If a child sins, they don't discipline him because he did evil in the sight of God but because he ruined the family name. They become so conscious of their image that their wayward son isn't welcome in church if he walks in with shaggy hair and wearing jeans. "Think of what you have done to *us*," they complain.

Our reputations *are* important, and each of us needs a proper self-image. But paradoxically, when we try to polish our reputation, we lose it; when we give it to Christ, we gain it. When we finally let the façade fall, we find freedom in our relationship with God and with one another. Image-building, the hallmark of worldliness, will finally be over.

Commitment to Christ means a radical change in perspective. Our priorities will be changed when we finally submit our will to God. And even then the struggle will not be over. Each day the initial commitment must be reaffirmed as new matters will be transferred to God's control.

Jesus is our example of obedience. We will never approach the measure of His commitment to do the Father's will. But our first feeble step toward freedom from the sins plaguing us occurs when we say, "Not my will but Yours." I've found it tough to say that and mean it. But it must be said—and meant.

## THE STRUGGLE FOR POWER

Let's suppose we have made the basic decision to submit ourselves to God. What happens next? We are to live by faith in dependence on the Holy Spirit. Again, Jesus is our example of how to operate while depending on the strength of Another. Jesus did nothing on His own. He let the Father work *through* Him. On numerous occasions, He reminded

His listeners that the Father was doing the work (John 5:17–19; 14:10). Even the words which He spoke were not His but had been given to Him by the Father (John 12:49). This quality of dependence illustrates the Christian life.

Many who read the Gospels are puzzled to find Jesus frequently went up to a mountain to pray and sometimes prayed all night. Since He was God, why did He need to be strengthened spiritually? Why did He repeatedly say He did nothing of Himself?

Although Jesus is God, He lived as man. Let us imagine a billionaire who decided to identify with the people in the poorest section of the city. He would walk to work with them, eat with them, and work at the same job. He would live on the wages he earned for the week. At any time, he could write a large check, live in a beautiful home, and lie in the sun every afternoon. But he doesn't. He doesn't depend on his wealth in the bank. He lives as the poor do, even though he's a billionaire.

Similarly, Christ, though having all the attributes of deity, lived as we do.[1] He voluntarily gave up the independent use of His attributes of deity and lived as God intended man to live—in total dependence on the Father. Christ is the last Adam; He lived as God intended the first Adam to live.

Jesus gave His disciples a clear command to follow His example. He said, "As the living Father sent me, and

I live because of the Father, so whoever feeds on me, he also will live because of me" (John 6:57). Christ intends that the same relationship He had with His Father be ours with Him. As He lived, so we are to live. This means we are to do everything in faith, abiding in Christ's strength, because without Him, we can do nothing that will count for eternity. Unfortunately, we sometimes reduce living by faith to financial matters, but everything we do—whether we eat, drink, or write a book on worldliness—must be done with an attitude of dependence on Christ who alone can please the Father through us.

The reality of Christ's power is brought to us through the power of the Holy Spirit. We will not be able to face the temptations of the world nor cope with the tensions of our age unless we are filled (controlled) by the Holy Spirit. He wants to display power through us, but His prompting is squelched through our unbelief and sin.

Today, we are bombarded with conflicting (and confusing) views of the Holy Spirit. Many Christians are convinced the answer to their emptiness is to have a crisis experience which will revolutionize their lifestyle. Until that "happening," they have accepted their defeat as inevitable. Those who have the experience (which may have a variety of labels attached to it) believe they have found the key to supernatural power. In the confusion, one fact is overlooked: any Christian can display the supernatural fruit of the Spirit to the extent that they live in dependence on the Holy Spirit who indwells them. In other words, there is no hidden secret nor additional spiritual experience we must have. Undoubtedly, we often learn dependence by means of a crisis experience; but the attitude of dependence, not the experience itself, is the key to spiritual victory.

Living by faith (dependence) is more easily talked about than done. I find it easier to explain how to live the Christian life than to do it myself for one good reason: My sinful nature balks at dependence and prefers independence. This is why growth and development are necessary for us all. We never get to the point where we can say "I've finally arrived."

One point needs emphasis: We cannot look to ourselves (our emotions, determination, or good qualities) for spiritual power. Supernatural power resides in Jesus Christ and the work which He has already *finished*. Because of our identification with Him, sins need not have control over us.

Let me illustrate. Because of a misunderstanding, I was angry with a man I thought had wronged me. My anger was sin. It affected my attitude not only to this man, but to everyone else. Even though I knew I was sinning, I had no control over my emotions. Even praying for victory didn't help. Then I remembered the objective fact of victory in Christ, the fact that *this* sin was already conquered on the cross. I realized victory was *legally* mine despite the way I felt emotionally. From that moment on, my anger began to subside, and later the bitterness was gone—much to my surprise! I found the greatest struggle was to trust the power of Christ even when I was coming apart emotionally.

God is powerful and wants to prove it in us. But that necessitates learning to live in dependence upon the Holy Spirit. Apart from that, failure is inevitable.

## THE STRUGGLE FOR FULFILLMENT

Student-teacher clashes are not new. The dialogues of Plato make it clear that the students of Socrates were greatly irritated by their demanding teacher. I was asked some time ago to help resolve the tension between a group of Christian students and their doctrine professor. During the discussion, one of the students summed up the mood of the world in a single sentence, "I don't see why I have to sit in any class that doesn't speak to my truth," he offered. "I have a right to skip any class that isn't meaningful to me."

The accepted philosophy of today is existentialism, which, in its popular form, emphasizes meaningful experience as the criterion for truth. Facts are considered irrelevant, except insofar as they "speak to my truth." Many who have "tried" Christ have become disillusioned because they didn't get a sense of meaningfulness or the "spiritual high" they had expected. In terms of speaking to their truth, some other substitute might do just as well. At least for a while.

Shouldn't the Christian life be more meaningful than any other experience, dogma, or religion? The answer depends on what you consider a meaningful life to be.

Let's look at Jesus once more. He reminded His weary disciples, "My food is to do the will of him who sent me and to accomplish his work" (John 4:34). The relationship with His Father was just as necessary as the food nourishing Him during those long walks in the blistering Palestinian sun.

The work the Father asked the Son to do was not exciting by itself. Washing the dusty feet of His disciples would not give anyone a "spiritual high," as many Christians constantly expect. But Jesus didn't complain. He didn't suggest it was disgraceful that God the Son be on His hands and knees.

To Jesus, it made little difference whether He was washing the disciples' feet or preaching the Sermon on the Mount. The *type* of activity didn't determine whether He was joyful or not. His joy was found in doing the will of God, and if that included washing feet, that was fine. All He cared about was that He could say, "And he who sent me is with me. He has not left me alone, for I always do the things that are pleasing to him" (John 8:29). That was enough to give life purpose and joy.

Undoubtedly, doctrine courses need improvement, churches should be more relevant, and Christian homes more exciting. But as long as we believe that the answer to fulfillment lies in changes in methods, techniques, and a more meaningful approach to Christian lifestyles, we haven't diagnosed our malady correctly. Nothing, not even classes that "speak to our truth" can be a substitute for finding fulfillment in God through the Scriptures He has given.

Here is the paradox: Jesus found the horror of the cross a joy, because whatever pleased the Father, pleased Him (Hebrews 12:2). The fulfillment (or meaningfulness) of the Christian life is not necessarily found in the experiences we have (many of them will disappoint us), but even tragedies can have a glimmer of joy when we have the faith to see God's purpose in it all.

St. Augustine observed that God made us for Himself and our hearts are restless until they find their rest in Him. Learning this is not easy. A thousand voices clamor for our attention, and a thousand causes vie for our support. But until we have learned to be satisfied with fellowship with God, until He is our rock and our fortress, we will be restless with our place in the world.

Whenever my life lacks meaning, it's because I am seeking fulfillment somewhere apart from God and His Word. Then God disciplines me to bring me back to Him.

I am only beginning to appreciate Christ's observation that to save one's life is to lose it, and to lose it for Him is to find it.

But slowly, God's promises are being translated into power. There is hope for Karen. There is hope for you and for me. That is encouraging.

## QUESTIONS FOR DISCUSSION

1. Discuss the struggle of the will. How may we allow God to control our lives?

2. Discuss the struggle for power. By what power are we to live?

3. Discuss the struggle for fulfillment. Read John 4:34 and discuss its application to this struggle.

4. When a meaningful life is lacking for a Christian, what is usually the problem?

CHAPTER FOURTEEN

# SO WHAT IF I AM WORLDLY?

Are the pressures Christians face in today's world new? Yes. And no. No other generation has had access to the benefits of the internet, but along with that, no other generation has had to live with the influence of the mass media (especially the toxicity of social media platforms), and easily accessible pornographic websites. Technology has created new anxieties, polluted our air, and ushered in a host of distressing changes. Along with the knowledge explosion has come a radical shift in the moral climate. Many Christians find it so difficult to cope with this generation, they hope for the Lord's immediate return. Of course, such a hope should characterize believers of all ages, but one senses that many Christians long for the rapture, not because of their intense love for the Lord, but because it symbolizes an escape from the distress of our age.

Yet, our problems aren't new. The components of worldliness, the struggles with the flesh and the devil, have always been part of Christian experience. Whether we retain our identity or are squeezed into the world's mold will depend largely on our individual relationship with God. For this reason, this book emphasizes our personal attitudes toward issues which clamor for a biblical answer.

Yet, as individuals, we must be concerned about the collective witness of the true church. John Donne reminded us that no man is an island; one man's victory or failure affects us all. This is especially true among believers because we are organically connected by the indwelling Spirit. Paul used the metaphor of the body to illustrate the interdependence of individual Christians (1 Corinthians 12:12–13). When one part of our physical body suffers, the other parts suffer; when one part accomplishes its duty, it is always a cooperative effort.

Have you ever seen a human hand severed from a body? It's gruesome. Yet, attached to an arm and connected to the nervous system, the hand is not only highly useful but beautiful too. The difference lies in its relationship to the body. Similarly, in Christ, *no individual is anything, cut off from the body.*

This interdependence results in a cooperative concern for the various parts of the body. What happens when you see an object hurtling through the air toward your head? Instinctively, your hand shields your head from the blow. Similarly, we as Christians are connected in Christ. When a Christian fails, we share their failure and care for their needs. When they're restored to fellowship, we rejoice with them.

We can't afford to believe it doesn't matter whether we are actively involved in the struggles against the world or whether we are drifting aimlessly with the tide. When we lose our passion for the church (Christ's body) and are preoccupied with our own concerns, our witness will be submerged. We will drown in the icy waters of indifference.

Recent trends in America encourage us. Many evangelical churches are growing rapidly. Scores of laypeople are beginning to see and embrace the challenge of witnessing for Christ in their vocations. The present emphasis on sharing and informal meetings (as opposed to the rigidity of some established churches) is healthy, if kept within New Testament guidelines. Furthermore, a greater number of evangelical books and movies are being sold now than ever before. And evangelicals are utilizing the internet and satellite communications more extensively year after year, from websites to podcasts to internet broadcasts. Sermons and books from great theologians (past and present) are available at the click of a button. These developments are cause for thanksgiving.

Yet the influence of the church in some segments of society is waning. In the face of moral perversion, political corruption, and purely secular attitudes, the voice of the church is lost, or at least muffled. Ironically, secular groups (e.g. anti-abortion coalitions) are fighting moral issues without much help from the evangelical church. Long ago we left the dynamic of the early disciples who were accused of turning the world upside down. Tragically, it often is the world which has turned *us* upside down!

If history repeats itself (as it often does, at least in principle), the witness of the church in America could eventually be obliterated.

An example of how this could happen comes from the records of history. From the second to the fourth centuries, Christianity spread rapidly throughout North Africa. Churches sprang up in rapid succession. A historian living in that day might well have guessed Christianity would become the dominant religion in most of Africa. It was here that Tertullian (known as the flaming thunderer of North Africa) and Augustine, the famous apologist, exerted their influence. Yet, the church in North Africa, which began with such high hopes, was later obliterated. A few centuries later, scarcely a trace of Christianity could be found. Why? What elements are necessary for a church to be absorbed by the world?

For one thing, the internal problems of the church distracted it from its mission of reaching the world. During persecution, thousands yielded to the pressure and compromised their faith. Later, many of these sought readmission into the church. The Novatians and Donatists agreed that these deserters should be denied acceptance by the church. A host of others disagreed. This issue split the church for more than a century. Augustine tried to bring about a reconciliation but failed.

Divisions in a church are sometimes necessary. The purity of the church has often been preserved by those who decide not to tolerate heresy or moral permissiveness. Yet, when the church is torn by its own squabbles; when divisions exist continually, defeat for both sides is almost inevitable.

The same is true in the local church. A church preoccupied with its own differences or torn by a schism is a good candidate for ultimate oblivion. In Ephesians 6, Paul describes the spiritual armor of the Christian. No provision is made for the Christian's back, not merely because he's never to turn and run in defeat, but also because it's assumed he won't be fighting his comrades. If all of his energy is used in family battles, he'll have neither the time nor the inclination to make an impact on the world.

The cure for this is compassion, understanding, and above all, love. As pointed out earlier, differences must be held without bitterness, self-righteousness, and pride. In this way, a church can work out its differences and exercise discipline without diminishing its impact on the world. Whenever we are preoccupied merely with our own survival, whenever we begin to entertain ourselves with our own quarrels, the end might not be too far away.

Another factor in the decline of the church in North Africa was the distinction made between the laity and the clergy. Iranaeus had taught that the apostles had appointed bishops as successors. Eusebius, the most famous of the early church historians attempted to list the bishops of several churches. Soon every town had its bishop. These men began to grow in power; they were in charge of the worship and supervised the entire life of the church within their territorial jurisdiction. Cyprian, Bishop of Carthage and martyr in the third century, held that he who was not in the church was not a Christian, and that outside the church there was no salvation. The belief then developed that the bishop had the authority to consecrate other bishops and ordain subordinate clergy. The New Testament teaching that every Christian is a priest before God was lost in an elaborate hierarchical system.

One of the greatest threats to the impact of the church is the belief that the clergy alone is responsible for spiritual matters. The clergy is hired to do the work of the ministry. Consequently, thousands of Christians don't even see it as their responsibility to serve God within the church and witness to the world outside of it. They believe attending church and listening to a sermon is the penalty they must pay for being a Christian. Beyond that, they have no vision, no ministry, no fulfillment. This is why the church cannot be revived without individuals being renewed. As long as people come to worship at a structure (a church building) without learning to live on supernatural power, the church will not survive for long. We are already seeing the carnal fruit of stagnant religion.

A sharp wedge between clergy and laity leads to the indifference of the laity; it also leads to the worldly attitudes of the clergy. In North Africa, the bishops began to use their spiritual authority to get political power. As the church and state became united, spiritual life was replaced with political arbitrations. Little wonder New Testament Christianity soon vanished in North Africa.

This book stresses the fact that Christianity is more than a set of regulations imposed upon believers. It is possible to fit into Christian patterns without discovering Christian power. Often our churches are simply functioning because of the momentum generated by faithful men and women of the past. When this happens, we will eventually lose our impetus. The challenge comes to each one of us to join in the battle against the world's deceptive influence and to march with supernatural power. Ministers and missionaries can't take our place in the struggle. Every believer (whether he realizes it or not) is involved in the conflict between good and evil, between God and the world. You and I dare not shirk our responsibility.

The church in North Africa declined for another reason: racial and social discrimination. A bishop of Carthage was consecrated in A.D. 311 by one who evidently was a traitor during the persecution. Another bishop was chosen by the Donatists. Yet, this split was not merely doctrinal, it was also racial. The Donatists were largely non-Latin; the Catholics were drawn from the Latin elements of the population. The Catholic element wished to preserve its power, and as a result, Latin was the language of the religious elite. The Bible was not translated into the language of North Africa, and by the time of the Vandal invasion in the fifth century, the light of the gospel was practically extinguished.

Ironically, modern Christians have not fully learned the lessons of history. When we appeal to one class or race to the exclusion of another, the gospel's impact will be diluted. Frequently, minority groups have considered the church as an enemy, or at best, an unconcerned friend. Why? Because our actions give the impression that Jesus died only for those who resemble *us*. Consequently, some racial or social groups believe Christianity—at least the Christianity they have seen—is not for them.

The church grows only in proportion to its penetration into the world. Without new converts, individual witnessing, and loving concern for people, its impact on the world is lost. There are no shortcuts to evangelism and growth. We can perpetuate the status quo with our own plans and initiative. But we can't change the world that way.

In A.D. 140, an anonymous Christian wrote a letter to Diognetus. In it, he described the Christian's relationship to the world:

> For Christians cannot be distinguished from the rest of the human race by country or language or customs. They do not live in cities of their own; they do not use a peculiar form of speech; they do not follow an eccentric manner of life. This doctrine of theirs has not been discovered by the ingenuity or deep thought of inquisitive men, nor do they put forward a merely human teaching, as some people do. Yet, although they live in Greek and barbarian cities alike, as each man's lot has been cast, and follow the customs of the country in clothing and food and other matters of daily living, at the same time they give proof of the remarkable and admittedly extraordinary constitution of their own commonwealth. They live in their own countries, but only as aliens. They have a share in everything as citizens, and endure everything as foreigners. Every foreign land is their fatherland, and yet for them every fatherland is a foreign land.... They busy themselves on earth but their citizenship is in heaven. They obey the established laws, but in their own lives they go far beyond what the laws require. They love all men, and

*by all men are persecuted. They are unknown, and still they are condemned; they are put to death, and yet they are brought to life. They are poor, and yet they make many rich; they are completely destitute, and yet they enjoy complete abundance. They are dishonored, and in their very dishonor are glorified; they are defamed and are vindicated. They are reviled, and yet they bless; when they are affronted, they still pay due respect. When they do good, they are punished as evildoers; undergoing punishment, they rejoice because they are brought to life. They are treated by the Jews as foreigners and enemies, and are hunted down by the Greeks; and all the time those who hate them find it impossible to justify their enmity. [Finally, in the conclusion of the letter, this Christian observed,] The soul, when faring badly as to food and drink, grows better; so too Christians, when punished, day by day increase more and more. It is to no less a post than this that God has ordered them, and they must not try to evade it.[1]*

Let us join hands with the Christians throughout the centuries who did not abandon the task to which God had called them. And if God be for us, who can be against us?

## QUESTIONS FOR DISCUSSION

1.  Read 1 Corinthians 12:12–13. Discuss the apostle Paul's metaphor of the body to illustrate the interdependence of individual Christians. What is the result of this interdependence?

2.  How would you describe the influence of the evangelical church on our society today?

3.  What elements contribute to the church's ineffectiveness in impacting its world for the cause of Christ? What is the cure for a lack of effectiveness?

4.  How is the Christian community to meet the challenge of impacting our world for Christ?

ERWIN W. LUTZER

# ENDNOTES

**Chapter Two**

1. Quoted in Howard G. Hendricks and William D. Hendricks, *Living By The Book* (Chicago: Moody Publishers, 2007).

**Chapter Six**

1. Although Paul says an idol "has no real existence" (1 Corinthians 8:4), he later asks, "What do I imply then? That food offered to idols is anything, or that an idol is anything? No, I imply that what pagans sacrifice they offer to demons and not to God. I do not want you to be participants with demons" (10:19–20). Perhaps this sheds some light on certain games sometimes associated with occult powers. Card games, for example, are often thought to have had such an origin. The point is that *anything* could be dedicated to the worship of demons, but the objects per se are totally neutral. Therefore, they should not be forbidden, unless some Christians did make occult associations with the practice. Then the Christians to whom the game has no such meaning should abstain so that the weaker Christians are not drawn back into their former way.

**Chapter Nine**

1. Harvey Cox, *The Secular City: Secularization and Urbanization in Theological Perspective* (Princeton University Press, 2013), p. 237.

2. Ibid., p. 240.

**Chapter Ten**

1. The Barna Group, "New Research Explores the Changing Shape of Temptation," (January 25, 2013), https://www.barna.com/research/new-research-explores-the-changing-shape-of-temptation/.

2. Neil Postman, *Amusing Ourselves To Death* (London: Penguin Books, 1985), 84.

3. Emily A. Vogels, Risa Gelles-Watnick and Navid Massarat, "Teens, Social Media and Technology 2022," Pew Research Center, August 10, 2022, https://www.pewresearch.org/internet/2022/08/10/teens-social-media-and-technology-2022/.

4. "Teens and Pornography," *Common Sense,* January 10, 2023, https://www.commonsensemedia.org/research/teens-and-pornography.

## Chapter Thirteen

1. As all illustrations of the incarnation, this one has its limitations. In some cases there is evidence that Christ did exercise the use of His attributes of deity, such as when He displayed omniscience. The relationship between His two natures has always been a mystery. But in general, this illustration shows how Christ, though fully God, lived as man.

## Chapter Fourteen

1. "The So-called Letter to Diognetus" in *The Library of Christian Classics* (Philadelphia, Westminster, 1953) 1:216–18.

.